SPIRITUAL LIVING

in a

SECULAR WORLD

Applying the
Book of Daniel Today

Ajith Fernando

MONARCH
B O O K S

Mill Hill, London and Grand Rapids, Michigan

First published in the UK in 2002 by Monarch Books,
Concorde House, Grenville Place, Mill Hill, London NW7 3SA.

Distributed by:
UK: STL, PO Box 300, Kingstown Broadway,
Carlisle, Cumbria CA3 0QS;
USA: Kregel Publications, PO Box 2607,
Grand Rapids, Michigan 49501.

ISBN 1 85424 578 3

British Library Cataloguing Data
A catalogue record for this book is available
from the British Library.

Book design and production for the publishers by
Gazelle Creative Productions,
Concorde House, Grenville Place, Mill Hill,
London NW7 3SA.

To

KUMAR AND PRIYANI

DULEEP AND SIRO

PRIYAN AND RUVENI

RAVI AND ANUSHA

with gratitude
from a brother who has
received so much
and
given so little
in return

Contents

Introduction   9

1 Getting Involved in a Fallen World
   (Daniel 1:1–8,17)   11
2 Living out Our Commitment in Daily Life
   (Daniel 1:8–21)   25
3 Peaceful Living in a Stressful World
   (Daniel 2:1–16)   37
4 It Happens in Small Groups *(Daniel 2:17–23)*   47
5 The Call to Personal Witness *(Daniel 2:24–49)*   59
6 Commitment: the Key to Heroism
   (Daniel 3:1–18)   71
7 God Is with Us *(Daniel 3:19–30)*   81
8 Confronting the Powerful with God's Power
   (Daniel 4:1–18)   91
9 Witnessing to the Powerful *(Daniel 4:19–37)*   101
10 People Who Don't Care about God
   (Daniel 5:1–31)   111
11 When Good People Come under Fire
   (Daniel 6:1–10)   121
12 Facing Trouble through Prayer *(Daniel 6:10–28)*   131
13 Keys to Powerful Prayer *(Daniel 9—10)*   143
14 The Mysterious Prophecies of Daniel
   (Daniel 7—12)   157
15 Living in the Shadow of the End Times
   (Daniel 7—12)   169

Endnotes   183

Introduction

It has been my privilege to work for more than 25 years with Youth for Christ volunteers and members of our church who are seeking to follow Christ at home, at school, and at the workplace. This book is written primarily for people like them.

The book of Daniel has many insights to help people who are seeking to obey Christ in a fallen world. I have shared these insights with many different audiences in Sri Lanka and abroad, culminating in a seven-part series at the ninety-seventh annual Maramon Convention in India. It is a joy to present this material now to a wider audience in the form of a book.

This book is written out of the conviction that the experiences of Daniel and his friends can equip us for spiritual living in an increasingly secular world. A Christian dental surgeon who heard some of the messages that resulted in this book said that being at the talks was like being at a counselling session where she received much helpful advice for the situations she faced. This is the result I wish for readers of this book. There are many excellent discipleship manuals for new believers today. My hope is that this book will be a discipleship manual not only for new but also for mature believers.

This book is not intended to be a commentary on

Daniel. It does not deal with every verse in the book, and its focus is primarily on applying to day-to-day life the teachings of Daniel gleaned through a careful study of its text.

In this study, however, I have been greatly helped by some excellent commentaries on Daniel. I found the commentaries of Gleason Archer, Joyce Baldwin, John Calvin, Alan Millard, Ronald Wallace and Edward J. Young especially helpful. Full bibliographical details of these and other commentaries used are given in the notes at the end of this book.

I wish to thank the many Christians who over the past years permitted me to enter into their lives by sharing their experiences and challenges with me. This has provided a background for much of what is written here. I am also grateful to my wife, Nelun, and my children, Asiri and Nirmali, and to my YFC colleagues for their support, prayer and sacrifice, without which this book could not have been written. My secretary, Helen Selliah, and assistant, Marudu Pandian, helped with many details relating to this book. Tim Stafford's friendship and counsel have been very encouraging. My correspondence with Jack Kuhatschek, editor of Lamplighter Books at Zondervan Publishing House, has enriched me greatly and done much to improve my writing skills. To all these people I wish to express my deep gratitude.

CHAPTER 1

Getting Involved in a Fallen World

Daniel 1:1–8,17

William Wilberforce was one of Britain's great social reformers. A member of Parliament for forty-five years, he is considered the most influential figure in the movement resulting in the abolition of slavery in Britain. He was also a committed Christian.

Wilberforce was converted to Christ a few years after he became a member of Parliament. His conversion came after a struggle. At a crucial time in that struggle he sought the counsel of the former slave trader, John Newton, who was then an Anglican priest and the author of many hymns, including 'Amazing Grace'.

Wilberforce felt that, if he became a Christian, he must be fully at God's disposal. He thought this would mean giving up his circle of friends and leaving the political arena. He felt he had to choose between Christ and the world. But he wanted both.

John Newton 'urged him not to cut himself out from his present circles or to retire from public life.' Two years later Newton wrote to him, 'It is hoped and believed that the Lord has raised you up for the good of his church and for the good of the nation.' Wilberforce took Newton's advice and stayed on in politics, even though at that time 'most evangelicals shunned public life as worldly.'[1]

Like Wilberforce, many Christians today struggle with the idea of combining commitment to God with involvement in the structures of this world. The book of Daniel tells the story of four people who lived and worked in a completely pagan environment. Their experience can teach us much today.

God is sovereign: even when evil triumphs
(1:1–2)

Daniel begins on a very bleak note. Jehoiakim, the king of Judah, had been defeated by Nebuchadnezzar, king of Babylon. Many Jews were taken to Babylon as exiles. And some of the articles from the temple of God were carried off to the temple of Marduk and put in the treasure house of Marduk (1:2).

Babylon was the place where, according to Zechariah, wickedness itself will be exiled (Zech 5:5–11). It was the centre of the worship of the much-detested god, Marduk or Bel (see Isaiah 46).

Yet the second sentence of the book of Daniel begins with the words, 'And the Lord delivered Jehoiakim' (v 2). The author claims that God is responsible for the defeat of his people and the desecration of the holy temple vessels!

What we see here is an expression of the strong belief that devout Jews had in the sovereignty of God. Even when evil seemed to be in control, God was actually in control and was working out his purposes. In this case, he was punishing the people of Judah for their unfaithfulness.

The theme that God is in control appears throughout the book of Daniel. The Lord knows what is happening, and even the trouble his people endure under evil people has been permitted by him and will fit into his ultimate plan.

Knowing that God is in control can keep us from being too discouraged as we live as Christians in difficult situations. It also gives us courage to be obedient when we are a small minority. God's sovereignty is a theme we shall refer to many times in the course of this book.

God can use natural abilities (1:3–5)

Verses 3 and 4 say that King Nebuchadnezzar looked among the Jews he had brought to Babylon for young potential leaders who could 'serve in the king's palace.' He had decided to enrich his kingdom by making use of the abilities of capable people from a minority race. One of his top officials, Ashpenaz, was given the job of choosing these people and grooming them for leadership.

Those who entered this elite group had to satisfy several requirements. They had to be 'Israelites from the royal family and the nobility — young men without any physical defect, handsome, showing aptitude for every kind of learning, well informed, quick to understand, and qualified to serve in the king's palace' (vs 4–5).

Keep in mind that these were the king's, not God's, requirements for leadership. There are some instances in the Bible where God used the natural abilities and resources of people for a special task that others were unable to do. But people from rich families or those who are physically attractive are not more important than others. God can use their natural talents and resources, however, as a blessing that brings glory to his name.

God can also use those with limited natural abilities and resources in significant ways. Throughout the Bible God chose weak, poor, uneducated, and physically handicapped people to do great things for him (see 1 Corinthians 1:26–29).

Even the great apostle Paul was accused of being '"timid" when face to face' with the Corinthians 'but "bold" when away' (2 Cor 10:1). They also claimed that 'his letters are weighty and forceful, but in person he is unimpressive and his speaking amounts to nothing' (2 Cor 10:10).

A mid-second-century writing described Paul as 'a man small of stature, with a bald head and crooked legs, in a good state of body, with eyebrows meeting and nose somewhat hooked.'[2] We can't be completely sure whether this description was accurate. But the Scottish archaeologist Sir William Ramsay felt that because it was such a vigorous and unconventional description it probably rested on good local tradition of what Paul looked like.[3]

So we need never be jealous of people who climb the social ladder because of their physical appearance, their talents, or their family connections. God has given each one of us special significance in Christ.

The unique role of the laity (1:6)

Verse 6 introduces the main characters of the book of Daniel: 'Among these were some from Judah: Daniel, Hananiah, Mishael and Azariah.' Through them God planned to do great things and to preserve his name during a bleak period in Israel's history. These people were not priests or prophets, who were the 'full-time Christian workers' in the Old Testament. They were young laymen.

How sad that, when we think of great men or women of God, we usually think of full-time workers. How sad that so few biographies are written about laypeople who distinguished themselves as God's servants in society. The Bible has a long list of heroes who were not, and never became, full-time workers. Abraham was an owner of livestock. Joseph was a government official. Joshua was an army chief. Ruth was a housewife. David, who was called 'a man after [God's] own heart' (1 Sam 13:14; Acts 13:22), was first a shepherd, then a warrior, and finally a ruler. Nehemiah was the cup-bearer of a Persian king. Esther was the queen of another Persian king.

Preachers are also important. They are able to set apart time to study the Word of God in a special way and teach it to others. We will soon see that Daniel and his friends had been greatly influenced by Jeremiah's prophecies. Yet it is primarily through laypeople that the world observes how Christianity is relevant to everyday life. Laypeople take the gospel into the classroom, the neighbourhood, the playing field, the office, and the marketplace. They show the world that the gospel of Christ really works.

Lay witness is particularly significant when the cause of Christ is under fire, as in the time of Daniel. Christians today are often accused of being narrow-minded, of trying to impose their views on others, of destroying the culture of the people, of lacking integrity, and of many other things. People end up having a stereotype of what Christians are like — and the image isn't very flattering.

Yet when people meet committed Christians who are honest, hard-working, concerned for others, and polite, they are forced to reconsider their opinion of the gospel. This winsome witness of laypeople challenges the false stereotypes of Christianity prevalent in society. We will see this happening over and over again in the lives of Daniel and his friends.

Unpleasant aspects of involvement (1:7)

One of the first things done to Daniel and his friends was giving them new names. Verse 7 says, 'The chief official gave them new names: to Daniel, the name Belteshazzar; to Hananiah, Shadrach; to Mishael, Meshach; and to Azariah, Abednego.' Alan Millard explains that 're-naming avoided the inconvenience of varied foreign names, helped to unify the mixed court, and displayed Babylonian lordship.'[4]

I do not think these young men would have been happy with having their names changed entirely for the convenience of the ruling people. D. S. Russell points out that 'to the Hebrew mind the name is much more than simply a "tag", an appellation. It contains within itself the "soul", the character of the man, indicating what he is in the depths of his being.'[5] The new names they received were related in some way to the Babylonian deities. The four young men also had to learn the pagan 'language and literature of the Babylonians' (v 4). But they accepted these unpleasant aspects of involvement because they had to be obedient to their superiors.

As you go into a society that has values different from yours, you may be asked to do things you don't like to do but that do not compromise your Christian principles. You may have to go to parties or receptions that are boring to you, and which sometimes are embarrassing because of the heavy drinking or the off-colour jokes. You cannot avoid polluting yourself at your workplace by hearing the profanity or the unedifying conversation of the people around you. You may have to sit for proficiency tests in subjects you think are of no use to you or you disagree with. But those are things that have to be done if you are to remain in the structure in which you seek to serve. So you do them even though you do not like to.

Daniel and his friends were not stubborn people who refused to do what they did not like. I know Christians who give religious excuses for not doing what they don't like to do. A person may refuse to go to a business party, saying it is against his principles to attend such functions. But the real reason is that he feels completely out of place there and wants to avoid feeling like a fish out of water.

Obedient involvement in society (1:8)

Although Daniel and his friends were willing to take on names and study projects they did not like, they refused to do things that went against their principles. Verse 8 says, 'But Daniel resolved not to defile himself with the royal food and wine, and he asked the chief official for permission not to defile himself in this way.' Later we see that the other three friends also joined Daniel in resolving to stay away from the food (vs 11–14).

Many reasons have been given for their refusal to eat the food and drink the wine. But nothing is conclusive. Perhaps they were afraid that the food had first been offered to idols. But, as John Goldingay points out, this would also have applied to the vegetarian food they ate. Perhaps they were afraid of eating foods declared unclean. Goldingay suggests that this may have been their way of symbolising that they were avoiding assimilation with the pagan practices. Therefore, though it seemed a trivial thing, the four men's actions had enormous implications.

This was a time of defeat for the people of God. They struggled to survive without giving in to practices the godly usually consider to be wrong. I think Ronald Wallace got to the heart of Daniel's attitude when he wrote, 'Under the circumstances of the exile, Daniel felt that a hopeless drift could be halted only by standing firm on the law, even in matters that at other times might seem inconsequential and strange.'[6]

Daniel and his friends chose to sacrifice pleasure for principle. But their sacrifice lifted up the name of God and gave courage to people whose confidence had been devastated by defeat. They showed that what others considered essential could be done away with for the sake of God's kingdom. And even in a time when God's kingdom seemed hopelessly defeated, these people, by their lifestyle of radical obedience, proclaimed that the kingdom was alive and well and displayed confident trust in the eternal God.

So these four young people were fully involved in the affairs of the world. They were willing to work hard on the pagan education they received. They accepted the pagan names they were given, but they would not compromise their principles. This gives us a hint about the way biblical Christians approach society. But first let us contrast the biblical approach with two unbiblical approaches found today.

The first approach to society is *isolation*. Some Christians say that because society is evil and against the kingdom of God they won't get very involved in it. They don't know much about what is happening in the world. They just survive and do church work.

But with that approach we cannot fulfil Christ's call to be 'the salt of the earth' (Mt 5:13). Salt cannot do its work unless it penetrates the substance on which it acts. Even God, the eternal Word, had to become flesh and make his dwelling among us (Jn 1:14) before he saved us. When praying for his disciples Jesus said, 'My prayer is not that you take them out of the world.... As you sent me into the world, I have sent them into the world' (Jn 17:15,18). With such words from the lips of our Master, we cannot isolate ourselves from the world.

The second approach to society is *accommodation*. Some Christians say that the way of the world is different from the way of the Bible. If they are going to succeed in society, therefore, they can't help accommodating themselves to it, even if that means breaking some biblical principles. They claim that this is particularly necessary when Christians are a small minority. When they are among Christians, they act like Christians. But when they are in the world, they act like everyone else.

Daniel and his friends are a great challenge to the practice of accommodation. They were fully immersed in a pagan culture. They worked hard and succeeded in society. But they did not compromise their religious principles. They challenge the position of those who say it is impossible to be totally committed to God and his principles in a fallen world.

Theirs is the approach of *obedient involvement*. Those who hold this view claim that because this world is created by God, the best way to live in it is by following the instructions of its Creator. By their life and witness they challenge the wisdom of the world when it opposes God's wisdom, and they demonstrate that God's way is indeed the best way. They go into the world with a confidence born out of their belief that God is its Creator. In order that they may know how the Creator intended them to live when he made them, they study his book of instructions, the Bible. Then they apply what they learn in their daily lives.

The importance of God's Word (9:2; Jer 29:4–23)

Daniel and his friends were deeply influenced by a letter the prophet Jeremiah sent to the exiles. That letter, being prophetic in nature, was the Word of God. Recorded in Jeremiah 29, it starts by affirming the sovereignty of God even in a time of national gloom: 'This is what the LORD Almighty, the God of Israel, says to all those I carried into exile from Jerusalem to Babylon' (v 4). The people are then advised to 'build houses and settle down; plant gardens and eat what they produce. Marry and have sons and daughters… increase in number there; do not decrease' (vs 5–6). They are asked, as far as is possible, to live their normal lives. God goes to the extent of saying: 'Also, seek the peace and prosperity of the city to which I have carried you into exile. Pray to the LORD for it, because if it prospers, you too will prosper' (v 7).

This attitude is a big contrast to the sentiments of other Jewish exiles in Babylon recorded in Psalm 137:1–4:

> By the rivers of Babylon we sat and wept
> when we remembered Zion.
> There on the poplars we hung our harps....
> How can we sing the songs of the LORD
> while in a foreign land?

Jeremiah's letter gives other pertinent advice. When things seem to be going wrong, the faithful may be tempted to look to astrologers or spiritualists for wisdom on what is going on. He alerts the exiles to this temptation and warns about false prophets and diviners (29:8–9). Then there is the promise of restoration and a glorious future for the people of God (vs 10–14). Next comes a strong word about the judgement that awaits those who have been disobedient to God (vs 15–23).

Jeremiah's letter provides the typical diet that one who feeds on the Word should receive. It has inspiration, promise, advice, and warning. We can see how it would sustain the four youths who sought to live in obedience under such difficult circumstances. Daniel 9:2 shows how this letter directly influenced Daniel's thinking. He says, 'In the first year of his reign, I, Daniel, understood from the Scriptures, according to the word of the LORD given to Jeremiah the prophet, that the desolation of Jerusalem would last seventy years.' This understanding prompts Daniel's famous prayer that we will discuss later in this book.

Daniel's experience demonstrates that if we hope to prosper as Christians while being involved in a fallen world, we must have a balanced diet of the Word of God. We will be bombarded constantly by ideas that oppose Christ's way. These ideas are so much a part of the environment that their influence on us is subtle and often not immediately evident to us. Therefore it is all the more important that we receive a corresponding influence from God. This will come if we saturate our minds with the Word of God.

Christians who went into society and stood firm in their commitment while achieving success testify to the high place the Bible has in their lives. Mark Hatfield, who served for many years as an American senator, writes, 'Since [the Bible] is the source of God's truth, we need to be saturated with it. We need to delve into it systematically, with enthusiasm, with curiosity, and with the willingness to apply God's will as it unfolds to us.' Then, after describing how we meet Jesus Christ through the message of the Bible, Hatfield says, 'This constant interaction with God, through the Scriptures, is the only way to maintain a healthy Christian life.'[7]

An eminent British physician, Dr David Short, who was the chief of Clinical Medicine in the University of Aberdeen, says this to his fellow Christian doctors: 'I think the low priority accorded to the reading of God's Word is one of the greatest sources of weakness of Christians in our generation.... Admittedly this takes time; and time is a rare commodity. But we can take time for anything we regard as important. If we only knew how our lives would be transformed if we made time to wait on God and read his Word, we should find the time somehow.' Dr Short says that one of the most important habits he learned from his father, who was also a doctor, 'was that of reading a part of the Bible every day.'[8]

Thinking biblically about secular issues (1:4,17)

The letter from Jeremiah was not the only thing Daniel and his friends studied. As part of their training they had to study the 'language and literature of the Babylonians' (1:4). They would, of course, have disagreed with much of what they learned. Joyce Baldwin describes this as 'a polytheistic literature in which magic, sorcery, charms and astrology played a prominent part.'[9] But if they were to progress in society, they had to study it whether they liked it or not.

Studying the thought-world of Gentiles was something the average devout Jew did not bother with. But this was because most Jews in Old Testament times did not have a missionary orientation. In contrast, Daniel and his friends sought to witness for God whenever they had an opportunity. Their knowledge of Babylonian thinking would have helped them a great deal in this witness. Paul also had a clear grasp of non-Christian thinking, and he would quote from the writings of the philosophers whom his hearers respected (Acts 17:28; Tit 1:12). That is one reason why he was such an effective evangelist to the Gentiles.

Today Christians encounter many beliefs that are opposed to the way of the Bible. We must stand against these. But often we know very little about these ideas. Therefore our reaction to them is more emotional than carefully reasoned. Our 'opponents' dismiss us, charging that we are fanatics who do not need to be taken seriously because we don't know what we are attacking.

Yet it is not enough to know the false teaching. We must know how to think biblically about it. In other words, we must seek to know what God thinks about it. This is what Daniel and his friends found out. Daniel 1:17 says, 'To these four young men God gave knowledge and understanding of all kinds of literature and learning.' They studied the pagan literature, but it was God who gave them knowledge and understanding.

This is one of the most absorbing challenges facing Christians today. We learn about science, culture, marketing, medicine, music, business, computers, or whatever. The authors of many of our textbooks and many of our teachers will not be Christians. But we must test the knowledge we receive with biblical thinking and decide which of it is acceptable, which of it must be modified, and which of it must be rejected totally.

Many years ago I heard Wesley Pippert, who was a senior and distinguished reporter with United Press International, share how he went about the process of thinking biblically about his profession. He said that early in his career he went through the Bible to see what it had to say about truth. Truth, of course, is the key feature in good journalism. Based on that study, he arrived at a list of some of the emphases and characteristics a Christian should report if he is committed to the biblical concept of truth. By doing this he was able, while maintaining an uncompromising Christian stand, to reach the top of his profession.

Similarly, those who want to go into a marketing or sales career would look for features that should characterise marketing done in a Christian way. They would, for example, decide that they should not tell lies to sell their products. They would decide that they will not try to persuade people to buy what they don't need. This is because, according to Christianity, it is wrong to waste money on unnecessary things.

Unfortunately, today we have reporters who are Christians, marketing people who are Christians, psychologists who are Christians and business people who are Christians, but few Christian reporters, Christian marketing persons, Christian psychologists, and Christian business people. So you may get a businessman who is a leader in his church, but who is very unreasonable in the way he treats his employees. You may get a Sunday School teacher who works as an accountant and is known to be lazy and impolite at her workplace.

There is an urgent need today to emphasise what Harry Blamires has called 'a Christian Mind'. In a very significant book with the same name, he says that we must learn to think about secular topics 'Christianly', that is, from a Christian perspective. He speaks of the schizoid Christian whose mind 'hops in and out of his Christian mentality as the topic of conversation changes from the Bible to the day's newspaper.'[10]

As you seek to develop the discipline of thinking Christianly about the things of this world, you should find some Christians who will be your accountability group. Daniel and his friends constituted such a group, as we shall see in chapter four. There is great value in learning from each other and having our ideas moderated by the wisdom of other Christians, for it is easy for our thinking to go astray when we grapple seriously with the world's ideas.

You may also want to read some books that have attempted to tackle issues facing Christians today. To start with, I would recommend *Decisive Issues Facing Christians*

Today by John Stott.[11] Stott, who is one of our most brilliant biblical expositors, is also a careful student of the world we live in. The book attempts to build a bridge from the Bible to the contemporary world. His insights on how preachers should relate the Bible to contemporary society have been expressed in his book *Between Two Worlds: The Art of Preaching in the Twentieth Century*.[12]

Let me end this chapter by urging you to take on the challenge of integrating biblical truth with your life — at home, at school, at work, and in society.

STUDY QUESTIONS

1:1–2   In what difficult situations in your life has the belief in God's sovereignty given you courage to persevere? Are you facing such a situation right now? Explain.

1:3–5   What instances do you know of where God used natural abilities for his glory? In what instances has the lack of natural abilities been used to display God's ability?

1:6   What five or six people have had the greatest impact on your spiritual life? How many of them are lay persons?

          Why do Christians usually think of 'full-time' Christian workers when they think of great Christians?

1:7   What are some of the things you need to do, that you do not like to do, but that do not compromise your Christian principles?

1:8   In what situations are you tempted to adopt the accommodation approach to society?

9:2   What steps are you taking to ensure that you have a balanced diet of the Word of God?

1:17   What key biblical themes should influence the way you think about your occupation — for example, truth in journalism or patient love in parenting toddlers?

CHAPTER 2

Living out Our Commitment in Daily Life

Daniel 1:8–21

Many years ago, a bishop of Uganda said about his people, the Baganda, 'If it came to it, I think the Baganda would be ready to die for Christ today: it is living for him that they find difficult.'[1] Many who go into the world with a desire to live for Christ soon find a myriad of challenges to their commitment, and they struggle to know how to come out victorious. Beginning in this chapter, we will see how Daniel and his friends put their faith into practice in the different challenges they faced.

The importance of clear-cut resolution (1:8)

Daniel 1:8 says, 'But Daniel resolved not to defile himself with the royal food and wine.' Right at the start of his training he made a firm decision. Taking some firm steps at the start helps us keep to our commitment as time goes on. For one thing, people get to know that we are Christians and that we have certain principles. Therefore, they expect us to act differently.

I did my undergraduate studies at a university that had only recently changed its status from a Buddhist seminary to a university. The vice-chancellor (president) was a Buddhist monk, and in my class only four Roman Catholics and myself bore the Christian label.

During the first few weeks, we had what was known as the 'Freshers' Rag' where we were made to realise that we were freshmen by those senior to us. I did most of the humiliating things they asked me to do. But when I was asked to do something that went against my principles, I politely refused, stating that I thought God would not be happy about my doing it. I was slapped and ridiculed about being an angel who had fallen down from heaven.

The news went round that a 'religious' person was among the freshmen. This helped me in many ways later. I learned to leave the scene of a conversation when it became obscene, and soon my friends expected me to do so. Later on, I would sometimes find myself laughing at an obscene joke that someone made. When my friends saw that, they would rebuke me, saying that is not the way Christians are supposed to act. Here were Buddhist people telling me how Christians should act! That stand taken at the start of my university career helped me to maintain a Christian testimony among my non-Christian friends.

We too must make specific and firm resolves about how we are going to flesh out our commitment in daily life. It is not enough for a busy executive to say, 'I will have a regular devotional life.' He needs to be more specific than that. He may need to say something like, 'I will have my devotions in the morning before I leave for work and, therefore, I will get up at 6.00am on every weekday.'

It may not be enough for a salesperson to say, 'I will remain pure.' She may need to say, 'I will not tell a lie to sell any item, even if I lose my job for not making enough sales.' Temptations to compromise sometimes hit us when we least expect them, and often a snap decision has to be made. Unless we have made a firm resolve before the time of temptation, we may not be ready to face it.

We all know of areas in our lives where we could be tempted to compromise. Let's make some clear-cut decisions about those areas and communicate them to the appropriate people without delay. Then, when we are tempted, it will be difficult for us to give in.

You may need to tell a Christian friend something like this: 'I am often tempted to tell lies in my job. I have decided that I will not tell even the smallest lie. If a lie slips out of my mouth, I will immediately speak to those who heard it and retract it, however humiliating that may be. Because I need help in this area from you, I will report regularly about how I have been faring with my tongue.' I have heard people say that habitual lying is one weakness that is almost impossible to overcome. But I am sure that if a habitual liar adopts the approach outlined above, he or she can break the habit with God's help.

The importance of politeness (1:8–9)

Daniel made a firm resolve not to eat the king's food or drink his wine, but when he communicated it to the chief official he did so with a polite and respectful request. Verse 8 says, 'He asked the chief official for permission not to defile himself in this way.' If he simply had stated that he could not eat the king's food because of obedience to the supreme God, he would have been correct. But when he 'asked the chief official for permission,' he was both correct and respectful.

The next verse says, 'God caused the official to show favour and sympathy to Daniel.' God was working behind the scenes to clear the way for his servant. Yet it is unlikely that the official would have shown 'favour and sympathy' if Daniel had not been polite and respectful.

God's ambassadors in the Bible typically show an attitude of respect for those of other faiths. When Paul was in Athens, 'he was greatly distressed to see that the city was full of idols' (Acts 17:16). The word translated 'greatly distressed' is used to describe an intense provocation. But when he expressed himself to the people of Athens, 'he reasoned' with them (Acts 17:17). The talk he gave to the leaders of that city was what John Wesley called a 'divinely philosophical discourse'.[2] Paul did not express the anger that was in his heart over the idols in Athens.

Non-Christians do not know the Word of God. So they must be persuaded about the truth of his Word. It was against those who claimed at least a nominal allegiance to the Word of God, like the rebellious Israelites and the Scribes and Pharisees, that the Old Testament prophets and Jesus spoke harsh words of rebuke. Our attitude to non-Christians who hold different views to ours is well expressed in 1 Peter 3:15: 'Always be prepared to give an answer to everyone who asks you to give the reason for the hope that you have.' Then Peter immediately adds, 'But do this with gentleness and respect.' These people don't understand biblical principles. They don't even claim to know our God. We can't expect them to think the way we think, so we seek to persuade them about the truth.

Parents of some of our YFC youth complain to me that their recently converted children have become very unpleasant after their conversion to Christianity. Their judgemental and disrespectful attitude to their non-Christian parents does nothing to commend the gospel to them.

When a Christian is at a party with non-Christians and is offered a cigarette, he could politely say, 'No thank you, I don't smoke.' But sometimes you hear people respond with something like this: 'Me, smoke a cigarette? Why, I wouldn't give a cigarette to my worst enemy!' That person unnecessarily alienates himself from one whose goodwill and openness may give a good opportunity to share the gospel.

Christians will always find that they are going against the tide. Therefore they must always be careful to maintain 'gentleness and respect'. We have seen a lot of opposition to the work of the gospel in Sri Lanka in recent months. Christians are being falsely accused of bribing people with financial incentives into becoming Christians. Many Christian leaders have decided that, if they are brought before authorities or threatened or questioned, they will always act with courtesy and respect.

The call to be polite applies to our attitude to people like the advocates of abortion and gay rights, to those who disagree with our principles at our places of work, and to those who hate all that is associated with the name of Christ.

Of course, we know that however polite and humble we are, when we start witnessing for Christ and sticking to our principles, some people will be offended. So a faithful Christian will invariably be unpopular with many people. This happened to Daniel and his friends, as we shall see. But let us pray that unpopularity will never come to us because we are disrespectful or impolite. Let us pray that the charge of arrogance that is often made against us is always totally unfounded.

Encountering misinformed concern (1:10)

Even though the official liked Daniel, he was afraid to implement his request. He told Daniel, 'I am afraid of my lord the king, who has assigned your food and drink. Why should he see you looking worse than the other young men your age? The king would then have my head because of you' (v 10). The official did not know about the power or the supremacy of God. He did not know that God will look after those who follow him, and that obeying God is the wisest thing to do. He thought in the way a normal person thinks and expected Daniel to get weak on such a restricted diet. He feared that if that happened he would get into trouble. He would probably be suspected of misappropriating the king's wealth by not giving the food to the people for whom it was intended.

Those who follow the way of the cross often encounter this type of reaction. Often it comes from people who really care for them, like their own family members. Christian parents see their children paying the price of costly discipleship and think that this will jeopardise their progress in society. The parents of most missionaries are disappointed about the decision their children made to go overseas and are afraid that they are going to be seriously harmed.

The legendary Dallas Cowboys (American football team) coach, Tom Landry, said that one of his players, Bob Lilly, heard him say that as a Christian he believed his relationship with God and his responsibility to his family came before football. Lilly's first reaction was to think that Landry had gotten the order mixed up. When he realised that he had meant what he said, he thought, 'Oh, no! We're never gonna win a football game!' He was, of course, wrong. Landry commented, 'Bob went on to make his own commitment to the Lord after he retired from the Cowboys, but when he joined us, he didn't understand how I could say such a thing.'[3]

The cross, by its very nature, looks like a sacrifice. With the eyes of faith, however, we see it as the gateway to life (Mk 8:34–38). But we shouldn't expect others to see it that way. We should not get disillusioned or bitter, therefore, when people don't understand or appreciate what we do out of our commitment to Christ.

We are the test of the gospel (1:11–15)

In verse 11 we find Daniel speaking 'to the guard whom the chief official had appointed over' him and his friends. For some reason he seems to be more open to a change from the normal diet than the chief official mentioned in the earlier verses. It seems that Daniel had endeared himself both to the chief and to his assistant, the guard.

Daniel must have realised that the officials would not authorise his request for a different diet unless they were sure they would not get in trouble by doing so. So he presented a reasonable proposal that they could accept even with their limited knowledge of God and his ways. He says, 'Please test your servants for ten days: Give us nothing but vegetables to eat and water to drink. Then compare our appearance with that of the young men who eat the royal food, and treat your servants in accordance with what you see' (vs 12–13). It is a plea for a ten-day test: a humble plea, as the words 'please' and 'servants' suggest. The guard 'agreed to this and tested them for ten days' (v 14).

When someone wants to buy a used car and is uncertain about its condition, he or she will take it on a test drive. The people of this world do not know much about our God. They need evidence that he is indeed who he claims to be. Many don't think it is worth following Christ. They will look to those who represent him on earth for evidence of the relevance and the desirability of the Christian way. We are the test of the gospel in this world.

Now we often say, 'Don't look at us; look at Jesus.' But before looking at Jesus, many people will first look at his followers to see whether what he has done for them makes Jesus worth looking at. Jesus himself knew this. So he said, 'Let your light shine before men, that they may see your good deeds and praise your Father in heaven' (Mt 5:16). Elsewhere he said, 'By their fruit you will recognise them' (Mt 7:20).

I have a German friend, Manfred Grossmueller, who used to come to Sri Lanka as a consultant for an irrigation project. Many years ago he and his wife, Margitta, went to a Billy Graham 'simulcast' rally that was held near their home. The novelty of the technology had a lot to do with their attending that meeting. Billy Graham was speaking from another European city, but the message was being screened simultaneously in many European cities, quite a novelty at that time.

After his message, Dr Graham invited those who wanted to commit their lives to Christ to come to the front of the auditorium. To Manfred's great surprise, his wife walked forward that day. He thought to himself, 'I'm done for! My wife has turned religious, and we won't be able to have fun anymore.' Yet he found that his relationship with her got better rather than worse after her conversion. He soon realised that he needed what she had. A few months after her conversion, he also gave his life to Christ. Christianity had passed the test. Today Manfred is an active lay leader in his church.

Daniel and his friends presented themselves to the unbelieving guard as a test of the benefits of obeying the God of Israel. God proved to be reliable, for verse 15 says, 'At the end of the ten days they looked healthier and better nourished than any of the young men who ate the royal food.'

Rethinking success (1:16-21)

With the test completed successfully, the guard is not afraid to grant Daniel's request. Verse 16 says, 'So the guard took away their choice food and the wine they were to drink and gave them vegetables instead.' These are healthy young men. Have you ever heard of a strong young man going on a Spartan vegetarian diet when plenty of rich food was at his disposal? And that was not just for a week or two but for three long years (v 3)!

Those living in affluent societies would find this type of deprivation difficult to imagine. The onset of the credit culture has made it possible for us to have what we want at just the time we want it, with a means to pay for it later. As a result, our catalogue of what is essential for a fulfilled life has expanded immensely in the past few years.

This trend has hit the church, too, and the results have been devastating. When most Christians decide about a vocation, the thought that comes to them first is how much money they will make. They have to pay for their educational loans quickly, get a 'good' car, purchase their own home in a 'good' neighbourhood and have enough money to wear 'good' clothes and 'good' shoes. In each of these cases 'goodness' is defined in a worldly way. Success also gets defined by these criteria.

There are many professions that do not pay well, but they perform a great service to the needy. Because Christians have defined success in purely worldly terms, they never think of going into such professions. We need Christians who will take the risk of going into banking schemes aimed at helping the poor. We need Christian men who will go into the teaching profession and be role models to children and youth coming from homes that have not had the privilege of a caring father. We need Christian full-time workers who will take working with youth, that forgotten segment of society, as a lifelong vocation rather than 'moving up' the ecclesiastical ladder the moment an 'opportunity' arrives.

Many missionaries from Western countries are doing a hopeless job of identifying with the people they have come to serve. They have an ineffective ministry because they never really get close to the truly needy people in that society. With their lifestyle they *can't* get close to them.

There is a lot of enthusiasm about missions today. But there isn't enough teaching about the simple and economically deprived lifestyle needed to minister effectively in a world where the majority of the unreached are poor. Unless this trend is reversed, we are going to see a whole crop of missionaries returning home frustrated after a term or two, wondering whether all the cost and effort of going to the mission field was worth it.

The plain teaching of Scripture is that many who achieved much for God's kingdom were deprived of some things the world regarded as essential for a happy life. Is it not significant that the Son of Man did not even have a place to lay his head (Lk 9:58)? This is the Saviour of the world who said he would give us 'life to the full' (Jn 10:10), and who said that when his joy is in us our joy is complete (Jn 15:11).

And this Source of complete joy never got married! History records that some of the most significant service to humanity was done by single people. Names like Amy Carmichael, Florence Nightingale, Henry Martyn, Sadhu Sundar Singh, and John Stott come immediately to mind.

Ruth Tucker, in her excellent book on the history of missions, *From Jerusalem to Irian Jaya*, has a whole chapter on single missionaries. She cites a report from a mission in Africa which stated that a single missionary lady does twice the work of a married man. Yet these missionaries never experienced the joys of married life and parenthood. In fact, Dr Tucker says that one of the major problems they faced was loneliness.[4] Singleness deprived them of some of the joys the world thinks are essential for a complete life. Yet if they had married, they would have missed God's best for their lives.

Our deepest fulfilment comes from our relationship with God. And in doing his will we deepen our tie with him. So being without some earthly pleasures is 'no big deal' for us, so long as we have the joy of the Lord. When we are tempted to feel insecure or deprived, the joy of the

Lord becomes our strength (Neh 8:10) and helps us to overcome that temptation.

Today there is a great need for us to emphasise the primacy of the joy of the Lord in the Christian life.[5] I hope you do not mind my saying that I got quite concerned when I came to the West. I found that when Christians talked about the blessings of God they mentioned things that most Christians in Sri Lanka could never have — like vacations in lovely spots, meals at fancy restaurants, cars, and new dresses.

Yet I do not think our people are less happy than those in the West, for the source of deepest joy has nothing to do with these things. So let's put these earthly things low in our list of priorities. Then if we are deprived of them we will not worry too much. This, in turn, will make us more available to do whatever God wants, for we will be willing to make whatever earthly sacrifice that calling entails.

So Daniel and his friends were not really deprived when they had to do without the king's choice food. They were obeying God, and because God was with them they would have had his joy. That is a privilege this world knows nothing of!

The chapter goes on to tell us that God honoured the commitment of these youths. They ended up at the top of their class. In fact, 'in every matter of wisdom and understanding about which the king questioned them, he found them ten times better than all the magicians and enchanters in his whole kingdom' (v 20). So we are not surprised to read that 'they entered the king's service' (v 19). The chapter ends by saying that 'Daniel remained there until the first year of King Cyrus' (v 21). He had over sixty-five years of distinguished service in the government.

God honoured the faithfulness of Daniel and his friends and gave them earthly honour. That, in turn, brought honour to God's name.

Of course, those who are obedient to God in society are not always assured of earthly success. But we can always be sure that God will be faithful to us. And he will honour his name through our commitment and will give us a reward that extends beyond this life into eternity.

STUDY QUESTIONS

1:8   In what areas of your life are you tempted to compromise? What clear-cut decisions should you make to help you overcome this temptation?

1:8–9   What unpleasant areas of conflict have you had with people of other viewpoints? How can it help to be polite in these situations?

1:10   Have you ever encountered misinformed concern from people who care about you? How did you respond to it?

1:11–15   In what ways could you be a test of the reality of the gospel to non-Christians?

1:16–21   How are your ideas of what is essential for life influenced by those around you? How have such influences hindered your joy? What should you do to resist such influences from the world?

CHAPTER

3

Peaceful Living
in a
Stressful World

Daniel 2:1–16

We sometimes hear Christians say that God is so good to them that they don't have a single problem to worry about. We wish we could say the same. But experience tells us that it won't be too long before all God's servants face some crisis. It is a pattern clearly set in Scripture.

The crises we face, of course, become new ways for God to show his ability. Experiencing his deliverance makes life exciting. But some of us may not sense that excitement when we are going through the crisis. Hebrews 12:11 says, 'No discipline seems pleasant at the time, but painful.' So even Christians shrink from their problems, struggling with fear and anxiety. This has often been my initial reaction to stress. But I have always come out of these trials realising how foolish I was to have been afraid.

We finished the last chapter on a triumphant note with Daniel and his friends placed in high positions in a pagan government. God had acted miraculously to bring them to such important positions. But the miracle-working presence of God did not make them immune to challenge and stress.

As we live in a fallen world that is hostile to God's ways,

we will face stress daily. In Daniel 2 we see two people who faced stress in totally opposite ways. One lost control of himself and became brutal, while the other remained calm and helped turn the crisis into something constructive.

Finding security (2:1–13)

Chapter 2 describes some dreams King Nebuchadnezzar had: 'In the second year of his reign, Nebuchadnezzar had dreams; his mind was troubled and he could not sleep' (v 1). He was afraid because in those days dreams were considered very significant. There were manuals on how to interpret dreams, and wise men conversant in this art would often be consulted.

Verses 2 and 3 tell us that Nebuchadnezzar turned to his wise men in his fear: 'So the king summoned the magicians, enchanters, sorcerers and astrologers to tell him what he had dreamed. When they came in and stood before the king, he said to them, "I have had a dream that troubles me and I want to know what it means."'

Verse 1 says that Nebuchadnezzar 'had dreams'. Now he himself says that he 'had a dream'. The change from the plural to the singular suggests that the same dream has recurred several times. The wise men make a very reasonable request. Verse 4 says, 'Then the astrologers answered the king in Aramaic,* "O king, live for ever! Tell your servants the dream and we will interpret it."'

Nebuchadnezzar's response to the astrologers is surprising: 'This is what I have firmly decided: If you do not tell me what my dream was and interpret it, I will have you cut into pieces and your houses turned to piles of rubble. But if you tell me the dream and explain it, you will receive from me gifts and rewards and great honour. So tell me the dream and interpret it for me' (vs 5–6).

---

* The original texts of Daniel start with the Hebrew language and switch to Aramaic from 2:4 until 7:28, after which it reverts again to Hebrew. The Semitic languages are so called because they are the languages of peoples said to have descended from Shem, the son of Noah. Included among these peoples are the Babylonians, Assyrians, Arameans, Arabs, and Jews.

It could be that Nebuchadnezzar did not remember the details of the dream. Or it could be that Nebuchadnezzar was testing the magicians to see whether they really had the powers they claimed to have. This may be why he says in verse 9, 'Tell me the dream, and I will know that you can interpret it for me.'

What an extreme reaction they got from the king! As we would have expected, the wise men were unable to tell what the dream was (vs 10–11). 'This made the king so angry and furious that he ordered the execution of all the wise men of Babylon' (v 12).

Why did he react in such an extreme way? He was a powerful man, firmly in control of everything that mattered in his kingdom. There was almost nothing on earth that could disturb his security. But here was something he could not control: a fearful dream that kept recurring. If he could not remember its details, that would have increased his anxiety. Because his security was in earthly things, he was rattled when he encountered something he could not control. Under these circumstances, this strong man felt weak and insecure. Therefore he asserted his power so that he could feel strong and in control again.

Extreme reactions to unexpected events are common in the lives of those who get their security from earthly things. And in this fallen world we can never find security from the things of this world. Perhaps you've seen a capable leader turn into a tyrant when he encountered challenges to the absolute authority he had enjoyed. That is because he got too much fulfilment from exercising his authority. When it was threatened, his insecurity was so great that he lost control of himself.

After violence became entrenched in Sri Lanka some years ago, a lot of uncertainty entered into our schedules. Programmes had to be cancelled suddenly after considerable work had gone into their preparation. Often we lived in fear of violence breaking out around us. Owing to these uncertain conditions, many Christian leaders with strong personalities left the country. Some said that they could not exercise their gifts properly under such circumstances. I believe their main problem was that they could not handle the insecurity of being unable to control their programmes and circumstances.

Sometimes a mother acts unreasonably when her child asserts his independence and makes an important decision without consulting her. The decision itself is a good one, but she is upset because she was left out of the decision-making process. She receives too much security from the fact that she controls her son's life.

A man tries to commit suicide when his girlfriend decides to break off their engagement. He had received too much security from his relationship with her.

A business executive gets so angry and unsettled after being overlooked for a promotion that he makes life miserable for the members of his family. He depends too much on earthly recognition for security.

As long as we live in this fallen world, we can never completely control the situations we face. Even Paul speaks of groaning along with the creation as it waits for its final redemption (Rom 8:22–23). Frustration is inseparably linked with living in a fallen world. Unless we have a deeper source of security and fulfilment than the things of this world, we are destined to a life of insecurity. Nebuchadnezzar was the most powerful political leader in the world at that time. But a dream was enough to make him lose control of himself and act like an insane man.

Responding under pressure (2:13–16)

What a contrast to Nebuchadnezzar Daniel is! Unlike Nebuchadnezzar, he really had something to panic about. Verse 13 says, 'So the decree was issued to put the wise men to death, and men were sent to look for Daniel and his friends to put them to death.' Yet his reaction shows nothing of the insecurity of Nebuchadnezzar.

'When Arioch, the commander of the king's guard, had gone out to put to death the wise men of Babylon, Daniel spoke to him with wisdom and tact' (v 14). By using wisdom and tact, Daniel was able to get an audience with the king — no small feat in those days of despotic monarchs! He asked the king 'for time, so that he might interpret the dream for him' (v 16). And the angry king was willing to wait a little longer before carrying out his sentence.

Daniel expressed the quality of 'gentleness and respect' that Peter says persecuted believers should have when they 'give an answer to everyone who asks [them] to give the reason for the hope that [they] have' (1 Pet 3:15). As Wayne Grudem explains in his comment on this verse, the answer must be made 'not attempting to overpower the unbeliever with the force of human personality or aggressiveness, but trusting in the Holy Spirit himself to persuade the listener.'[1]

I have a friend who is a pastor in a Muslim country. He has often had threats on his life because of his evangelistic activity. One day a group of twenty fanatical, young Muslims came to his house and angrily demanded that he come out. My friend came out realising that he was at death's door. While his wife prayed inside, he spoke politely to the youths, offered them chairs to sit on and said he would like to discuss with them their cause for agitation. They angrily refused to talk to him. He offered to bring them some tea to drink, in keeping with the way visitors are treated in our part of the world. Again they angrily refused.

With these youths was a learned Muslim scholar. He called the boys to himself and told them to contrast their behaviour with that of the Christian pastor. He told them how rude they had been to the pastor. (Clergy of all religions are usually treated with much respect in the East.) Then he reminded them of how polite the pastor had been, of how he had even offered them chairs to sit on and tea to drink. He told them that they should be ashamed of themselves, and he asked them to apologise to the pastor. This they did, each one individually, after which they quietly departed. My friend and his wife immediately knelt down and thanked God for delivering him from the jaws of death.

When we live for Christ in a world that is hostile to his ways, we will often face situations that ordinarily would cause us to panic or to lash back excitedly. But what is needed at such times is wisdom and tact. Daniel was zealous for God and his principles. He stood up for what was right even at the threat of his life. But along with his zeal he had a wisdom that caused him to be tactful in sensitive situations. Proverbs 19:2 says, 'It is not good to have zeal without knowledge, nor to be hasty and miss the way.' God has given us brains, and we need to use them to decide on the wisest way to respond to the challenges we face.

Ecclesiastes 3:7 says, 'There is... a time to be silent and a time to speak.' If a Christian receives an unjust letter of reproof from his employer, it may be best for him to restrain his immediate impulse to proclaim his innocence in public. Making a big fuss about the letter might harden the attitude of the employer and complicate the process of resolution.

The best thing for him to do may be to politely meet the employer and explain the facts to him. Often we respond to such problems by making counter accusations and deepening the rift. Counter accusations may temporarily help retrieve our lost pride. But in the long run they are destructive.

Finding peace in the storm (2:13–16)

How was Daniel able to remain calm when he heard that he was going to die? He trusted in a God who was bigger than the problem he faced. He knew that God looks after his own, and that if God is faithful he had nothing to fear. This is the security of those who trust in the almighty God. A Jewish song of praise says,

> You will keep in perfect peace
> him whose mind is steadfast,
> because he trusts in you.
> Trust in the LORD forever,
> for the LORD, the LORD, is the Rock eternal.
> (Is 26:3–4)

Because God is sovereign, we are at peace even in the midst of great turmoil. 'We know that in all things God works for the good of those who love him' (Rom 8:28).

Bernard Gilpin was an Anglican preacher in the sixteenth century during the reign of Queen Mary, a monarch who put many preachers to death. He was arrested and was being taken on horseback to London to be tried for preaching the gospel. As he travelled to what was certain death in the flames, he frequently kept remarking, 'Everything is for the best.' His captors made fun of this remark.

On his way, he fell from his horse and broke his leg. This made his captors especially merry. But Gilpin quietly remarked, 'I have no doubt but that this painful accident will prove to be a blessing.' He was delayed because of the injury and arrived in London some days later than he had been expected. When they reached the prison, they heard the bells ringing merrily in the city. They asked the meaning and were told, 'Queen Mary is dead, and there will no more be burning of Protestants!' 'Ah,' said Gilpin, 'you see, it is all for the best.'[2]

So a Christian can say, 'Everything is for the best,' as he faces a redundancy from his company that is struggling because of the economic recession, for he knows that the One who owns the cattle on a thousand hills is with him (Ps 50:10).

A young lady can say, 'Everything is for the best,' when her fiancé suddenly breaks his engagement to her, for she knows the promise of God, 'I will never leave you nor forsake you' (Josh 1:5).

A father of young children can say, 'Everything is for the best,' after he finds out he has cancer, for he knows that the Great Physician, who can heal him if he wishes, has promised, 'My grace is sufficient for you' (2 Cor 12:9).

Scripture asserts God's sovereignty in page after page. And that sovereignty is directed for our benefit. Isaiah 26:3 says we will be kept in perfect peace if we trust in this sovereign God. To trust in this way, we must feed on God's Word daily so that its message of sovereignty will impact our hearts daily. That impact will help us overcome our temptations to doubt God and panic in difficult situations.

I must add that the truth of God's sovereignty over our circumstances may not come to each of us immediately when we face a crisis. Often our natural reaction is to be afraid and anxious. There are numerous examples of God's great servants who were distressed over what they were encountering. Elijah told God he wanted to die (1 Kings 19:4). Jeremiah wished he had never been born (Jer 15:10; 20:14–15). Asaph said that it was in vain that he had lived a righteous life (Ps 73:13).

In those times they acted without applying the promises of God to their situations. Yet these people did not proclaim their doubts in public and let others suffer because of their struggles. Instead they went to God and sought an answer. And answers did come to each of them.

So when we are troubled by the circumstances we face, we must go to him and battle with him, expressing to him our fears and our doubts. In his own gracious way he will break through to our troubled hearts, apply the promises in his Word to our situation and restore our peace. When we realise the way the promises apply to our situation, we will find our fears challenged by the sovereignty of God and finally banished.

STUDY QUESTIONS

2:1–13   What are some situations you face that you cannot control? What is your natural reaction to them? How do you react when you get God's perspective on that situation?

Have you seen extreme reactions similar to those described in this chapter? Explain.

2:13–16   What difficult situations have you faced where acting with wisdom and tact has saved the situation for you? Or where the lack of wisdom and tact caused (or could cause) serious problems?

Why do you think many Christians who believe in God's sovereignty with their intellect behave as if they don't believe it when they encounter difficult situations?

Though many Christians do not let God's peace control them the moment they face a crisis, often the perspective of God's sovereignty breaks through subsequently. What things have helped this perspective to break through in your life? What disciplines or actions do you need to adopt to help you develop this perspective when you face a crisis?

Often the perspective of God's sovereignty comes through an unmistakable intervention of God into our lives. Have you experienced such interventions? Explain.

CHAPTER

4

It Happens
in
Small Groups

Daniel 2:17–23

Friendship is the greatest of worldly goods. Certainly to me it is the chief happiness of life. If I had to give a piece of advice to a young man about a place to live, I would say, 'Sacrifice almost everything to live where you can be near your friends.' I think I am very fortunate in that respect.[1]

This is what thirty-seven-year-old C. S. Lewis, an Oxford English literature don and author of three books, wrote to his lifelong friend, Arthur Greeves. Lewis lived another twenty-seven or so years. Since the time of that letter, over fifty more books of his have been published.[2] He has been justifiably called 'the greatest lay champion of basic Christianity in the twentieth century.'[3] Yet those who have studied the life and work of Lewis say that his circle of friends had much to do in forming his great insights that have influenced so many people. Lewis gave a significant portion of his time to enriching friendships.

A key feature of the book of Daniel is the friendship among Daniel and his three friends. No study of their perseverance against so many odds would be complete without reference to their friendship. We are at a good point in their story to look at this friendship.

The importance of sharing with friends (2:17)

Daniel has succeeded in getting the king to delay carrying out the death sentence against the wise men. Daniel 2:17 says, 'Then Daniel returned to his house and explained the matter to his friends Hananiah, Mishael and Azariah.' These four people are under the sentence of death, and it is a scary time for them. It would be easy at such a time to act rashly. By sharing the problem as friends, they prevent each other from taking such a step.

Friends help us to respond wisely when we are attacked. It is difficult to keep our head at such times. We want to lash out in order to find a quick solution to our problem. But often our rash reactions do more harm than good.

A person may resign from a position she is well suited for after being rebuked for making a mistake. Another may write letters to a wide range of people, answering a criticism made against him by one person. A whole group of people are unnecessarily dragged into an issue with which they have no connection. Consequently the resolution to the problem becomes so much harder to effect. A person may choose to fight an 'enemy' when the wisest thing to do is to ignore his blows.

The advice of friends helps us avoid such rash reactions. Proverbs 12:15 says, 'The way of a fool seems right to him, but a wise man listens to advice.'

Friends show us when we are getting out of line. It is easy to compromise our principles when we are involved in the affairs of this world. When Hananiah, Mishael, and Azariah faced the blazing furnace for not bowing to the image Nebuchadnezzar made, they must have been tempted to bow down, especially when they were given a second chance to save their lives. They could have rationalised by arguing that a simple act of bowing down once was not a 'big deal' and that they could do more for God if they lived on. But the presence of the other two would have given each one the courage to withstand the temptation to compromise.

I have seen many people who were committed Christians in their youth gradually drop their Christian principles after they start working. It does not come suddenly. One compromise leads to another until they are completely won over to worldliness.

How easy it is to slip into using dishonest business practices in order to sell a product. And that sale may be just what is needed to prove to our superiors that we are good at our job. How easy it is to begin sharing at a deep level with a non-Christian colleague of the opposite sex, only to find that after some time we have fallen in love.

A relationship of spiritual accountability with a few Christians may help you overcome such temptations to compromise. Yet today people don't like to have others 'prying' into their affairs. By protecting their privacy they miss out on one of God's rich ways of ministering to them.

Our friends help us keep our priorities as we strive for success in society. Young adults particularly have a problem with priorities in their early years of employment. They have to demonstrate their abilities in a very competitive environment, and that is not easy. So they are tempted to neglect other important aspects of life, like family, worship, and fellowship. It is common to see their involvement in these areas becoming less and less as they get more and more involved in their jobs. Our friends have a way of challenging this trend and the false sense of values that lies behind it.

Hebrews 10:23–25 speaks to this very issue. In verse 23 the author urges us to persevere without compromise: 'Let us hold unswervingly to the hope we profess, for he who promised is faithful.' The next verse encourages us to help each other persevere: 'Let us consider how we may spur one another on toward love and good deeds.'

The word translated 'spur' is a strong word that is sometimes translated as 'provoke'. In other words, our friends should challenge us when we give low priority to Christian service ('love and good deeds').

Next the writer of Hebrews tackles a problem many of

us face when we get very busy in our professions: 'Let us not give up meeting together, as some are in the habit of doing, but let us encourage one another' (v 25). However busy we may be, corporate worship and fellowship must not be neglected because they are a high priority for any Christian.

Our friends help us to persevere in our chosen calling when we encounter formidable obstacles. The call of God sometimes takes us along paths that do not win prestige and wealth on earth. The temptation to give up becomes especially strong when we compare ourselves with others who seem to have an easier time. As the years go by, we may grow weary of paying the price our call requires. Our friends can help us keep our eyes on the real value of what we are doing when doubts arise.

When I was a student in high school, I had the formidable task of studying for the university entrance examination. Only a very small percentage of those who attempt this examination enter university in Sri Lanka, as very few places are available. For me this meant studying into the night for a period of many months. Because I was already intent on going into vocational Christian ministry, I found settling down to study very difficult. Many people going into ministry do not bother to go through the rigours of this examination in Sri Lanka. But I felt that God wanted me to take this route.

Every few days I would think of giving up my attempt to enter the university. But I did my studies with a Christian friend who rebuked me whenever I mentioned giving up. He too often thought of giving up. Then it was my turn to rebuke him. My friend helped me to succeed in the examination.

I spoke in the first chapter of William Wilberforce, who battled in the British parliament to abolish the slave trade in Britain. He introduced his first motion for abolition in 1789. Parliament passed the abolition bill only in 1807. In practice, slavery was abolished in the British Empire only in 1833, the year of his death. It was a long and bruising battle. This is how Richard Lovelace describes it:

Some of the leaders lost their health and their fortunes in the course of it. The opposition vilified 'the saints' [those who advocated abolition] as advocates of financial suicide of the British Empire; the attack on an institution which seemed so fundamental to the economic base of England appeared either as treason or insanity.[4]

While Wilberforce was the name behind the struggle, he was supported by a group of Christians, who were given the unfortunate name 'the Clapham Sect', because they lived near Clapham. This group of wealthy aristocrats were also committed Christians and practised a close community life with each other. They provided the encouragement and backing Wilberforce needed to persevere in this hard work. When Wilberforce was getting old, one member, Zachary Macaulay, provided him with the facts and figures he needed for his battles.[5] They were a praying group and 'habitually spent three separate hours in prayer daily.'[6] This is how one author describes the group:

Living mostly in one village and working in London, they were able to think, talk and eat together with a minimum need of correspondence and formality. On social and moral questions they came to be of one mind, even though on political questions they frequently differed among themselves. Their very homogeneity and singleness of purpose made them a greater force in English political and social life than any other body before or since.[7]

Certainly all of us cannot be a part of a group that makes such an enormous national impact. But every Christian involved in a difficult profession in society should have some group that will encourage him or her to live the Christian life amidst the many obstacles they will face. If those involved in society hope to maintain a healthy Christian witness, it is essential that they cultivate relationships of fellowship and accountability with other Christians.[8]

The excitement of united prayer projects
(2:18–19)

After Daniel shared the problem with his friends, 'He urged them to plead for mercy from the God of heaven concerning this mystery, so that he and his friends might not be executed with the rest of the wise men of Babylon' (v 18). Their prayer was answered, and 'during the night the mystery was revealed to Daniel in a vision' (v 19).

United prayer projects are among the most rewarding aspects of Christian community life. We have already said that this was an important part of the Clapham sect to which Wilberforce belonged. Community prayer is exciting because we pray to a prayer-answering God. The book of Acts shows what an important place prayer had in the early church. Before Pentecost 'they all joined together constantly in prayer' (Acts 1:14), and as a result they saw the mighty descent of the Spirit in revival fire at Pentecost (Acts 2). We are told that following that event the church members 'devoted themselves... to prayer' (Acts 2:42).

In a crisis there is nothing better for a group than to pray together. Acts 4 records the first instance of the church being persecuted. Peter and John report to the church about their trial and the outlawing of evangelism. 'When they heard this they lifted their voices together in prayer' (4:24) and God answered miraculously: 'After they prayed, the place where they were meeting was shaken. And they were all filled with the Holy Spirit and spoke the word of God boldly' (4:31).

When Peter was thrown into prison in Acts 12:5, 'the church was earnestly praying to God for him.' After his miraculous release, he went to Mary's house, where 'many people had gathered and were praying' (v 12).

Acts 13:2 says that believers in Antioch 'were worshipping the Lord and fasting' when the Holy Spirit told them, 'Set apart for me Saul and Barnabas for the work to which I have called them.' After their commissioning, the church itself 'fasted and prayed... placed their hands on them and sent them off' (v 3).

That is how the first formal missionary team to the

unreached was commissioned. Thousands of such teams have since gone to the unreached, and they represent what is possibly the most exciting movement in history.

Scripture affirms that exciting things happen when people get together to pray. We can pray for our burdens, our needs, and our weaknesses. We can ask God together for guidance on issues we face. We can pray for protection from our enemies. We can pray for purity in the face of temptation. We can pray for revival. We can ask God to deliver us in times of danger, as in the case of Daniel and his friends.

When Daniel went to his friends, he '*urged* them to plead for mercy from the God of heaven' (2:18). While Peter was in prison, 'the church was *earnestly* praying to God for him.' Often this sense of earnestness or urgency in prayer precedes a great outpouring of blessing from God.

We once found that prayer was taking a low place in the community life of our ministry. At a meeting of our leadership team we discussed possible causes. A colleague mentioned that our lack of urgency in prayer was probably because we were not facing any major crises in our work at that time.

I mulled over that for some time and was struck by the fact that we did face many urgent crises. There was the crisis of millions of lost people in our land and in the rest of the world. That crisis troubled Paul so much that he was willing to be cursed and cut off from Christ if that would bring salvation to his people (Rom 9:1–3). That crisis motivated him to pray for the salvation of the Jews (Rom 10:1). I also realised that we faced the crisis of numerous young people reached through our ministry who were living out of fellowship with God. Then there was the crisis of a nation being destroyed by violence and strife. There was also the crisis of thousands of hungry and needy people in our land.

I realised that the problem was not the absence of a crisis, but that our consciences were dulled to the needs around us. We had lulled ourselves to a spiritual stupour that robbed us of urgency. Anyone near to the heart of God should also be so sensitive to God's concerns that he or she lives daily in an attitude of earnest prayer.

Any group battling for God's kingdom and against the kingdom of evil will soon realise that prayer is one of the most important battle strategies. Paul closes his discussion on spiritual warfare in Ephesians 6 by urging his readers to pray (v 18). He first describes the nature of the battle (vs 10–13). Then he lists 'the full armour of God' that we are to put on (vs 14–17). We would have expected him to end his discussion by saying, 'Now go and fight!' But instead he said, 'And pray....' But he *was* urging his readers to fight, for prayer is a form of warfare. Paul used battle language to describe prayer in Colossians 4:12 when he said, 'Epaphras... is always wrestling in prayer for you.'

During the parliamentary battle for the abolition of slavery, 'Christians all over England united in prayer on the eve of critical debates.'[9] Wilberforce's inspired oratory did much to win the battle. But he was undergirded by the prayers of God's people. And God used that also as a means to victory in the battle.

In Daniel 2 the initiative to pray is taken by Daniel, the leader, who 'urged [his friends] to pray for mercy.' The leader's initiative is a key to the prayer life of any group. There are so many things to discuss when we meet, so many challenges we face, that it is easy to neglect prayer, or simply to tag it on as a ritual item at the start or at the end of the meeting. The leader must ensure that prayer is given priority.

I have led Christian groups for many years, and I must confess that often, almost unnoticed, prayer has gotten sidelined and almost dropped from the agenda of our meetings. Then somebody notices this and remedial steps have to be taken. Recently I have been very concerned at the number of Christian leaders who have told me they hardly pray with their spouses. I feel it is a law of the spiritual life that unless the prayer life of an individual, a couple, or group is carefully cultivated, and the prayer time jealously guarded, that group or individual will slide into relative prayerlessness and ineffective ministry.

The joy of community praise (2:19–23)

After God answers Daniel's prayer and reveals the mystery of the dream to him, his first reaction is to praise God. Verse 19 says, 'Then Daniel praised the God of heaven.'

He literally stopped everything to give himself to praise. All the wise men in Babylon were in suspense, wondering what would become of them. Daniel and his friends now had the answer to the problems of all these people. But they did not immediately dash out of their houses to proclaim the good news. They did not start getting ready for Daniel's audience with the king. All that could wait. First they had to praise God. Praise and thanks to God was a priority to this group.

Praising God together is one of the most enjoyable aspects of Christian community. A group may be in a rut and have lost its freshness. The meetings drag on without much purpose, and members attend more out of a sense of duty than of delight. Then somebody says, 'Let's spend some time in worship.' Hymns and songs of praise are sung, testimonies of God's goodness are shared, passages of Scripture are read, and prayers of praise are lifted to heaven. You feel you have experienced ecstasy!

The Bible gives a very high place to praise. What is not so well known is that much of biblical praise was done in community.[10] Of course, there are many instances of individual praise. Some of our highest moments of ecstasy are when we spend time alone with God in thanksgiving and praise. But when the faithful met in the Bible, one of the things they did most often was to thank and praise God. Every glimpse we get of heaven has its inhabitants praising in community. Psalm 95:1–2 has a word all groups of Christians should heed:

> Come, let us sing for joy to the LORD;
> let us shout aloud to the Rock of our salvation.
> Let us come before him with thanksgiving
> and extol him with music and song.

Daniel's prayer (vs 20–23) is a good model of biblical

praise. The first line is a proclamation: 'Praise be to the name of God for ever and ever.' Next Daniel mentions the two attributes of God that were evident in his answer to their prayer: 'Wisdom and power are his.' God's omnipotence is also described: 'He changes times and seasons.' He even controls the events of political history — including the fortunes of King Nebuchadnezzar: 'He sets up kings and deposes them.'

Daniel also focuses on God's action in revealing the dream: 'He gives wisdom to the wise and knowledge to the discerning. He reveals deep and hidden things; he knows what lies in darkness, and light dwells with him.' Finally Daniel thanks and praises God for all that he did: 'I thank and praise you, O God of my fathers: You have given me wisdom and power, you have made known to me what we asked of you, you have made known to us the dream of the king.'

Daniel used a gracious act of God to reflect on his nature and ways and that reflection forms the content of his praise. That is what praise is: looking at what God has done, reflecting on what that tells us about God, and expressing those reflections in words.

In this chapter we have learned why all who seek to be obedient to God in this fallen world should belong to a group of Christian friends. We have looked at some of the things they should do when they are together. Let me close this chapter by urging you to become part of such a group or, if necessary, to start one yourself. It could add a vital and enjoyable dimension to your Christian life!

STUDY QUESTIONS

2:17   Why do most people find it difficult to maintain close friendships today?

Why are people reluctant to share their struggles with others? How can this reluctance be overcome?

What adjustments need to be made to your lifestyle and schedule to give priority to spiritual accountability with a few Christian friends?

Can you think of instances when your close friends helped you persevere in a difficult task or helped you avoid a serious pitfall? Explain.

2:18–19   What place does prayer have in the group to which you belong? Does the leader need to do something to help give priority to prayer? Explain.

2:19–23   What place does praise have in the group to which you belong? What can be done to give praise its proper place?

Why do Christians often neglect to praise and thank God after they have received answers to specific prayers?

Using Daniel's prayer as a model, write down a prayer of praise for a prayer request God granted you.

CHAPTER

5

The Call to
Personal Witness

Daniel 2:24–49

Williamilliam Wilberforce has been mentioned a number of times in this book. That is because there are many parallels between his life and Daniel's. Like Daniel, he went into society and achieved great things. Like Daniel, he was committed to a group of friends, with whom he prayed in times of need. Like Daniel, he maintained his firm commitment to God to the end.

Another feature Wilberforce had in common with Daniel was his desire to share his faith with others. This is how a biographer describes that desire:

> Very early in his own pilgrimage Wilberforce set out to bring his friends to Christ. He would agonise about them in his diary and his prayers, he would think out phrases or subjects ('launchers', he termed them) which might turn the talk to religion, whether at table or tête-à-tête. He adapted his approach to his friends' characters.[1]

Some years ago I did some informal interviews with vibrant Christians who worked in non-Christian surroundings. I wanted to know what helped them to maintain their commitment. I was surprised at how many mentioned that attempting to witness for Christ at every possible opportunity helped them to maintain their Christian commitment in their jobs.

Daniel used his audience with King Nebuchadnezzar as an opportunity to talk about God.

Turning situations into openings for personal witness (2:24–30)

After praising God for revealing the mystery of the dream, 'Daniel went to Arioch, whom the king appointed to execute the wise men of Babylon, and said to him, "Do not execute the wise men of Babylon. Take me to the king, and I will interpret his dream for him"' (v 24). When he was brought there, 'the king asked Daniel..., "Are you able to tell me what I saw in my dream and interpret it?"' (v 26).

Daniel stands before a king who is in such a rage that he is ready to kill all his wise men. If I were in Daniel's situation, I would be extremely nervous. Under such circumstances we would expect Daniel to answer, 'Yes,' and to quickly proceed to his interpretation in order to save his life.

Instead, he uses the opportunity to witness about God. He says, 'No wise man, magician or diviner can explain to the king the mystery he has asked about, but there is a God in heaven who reveals mysteries. He has shown King Nebuchadnezzar what will happen in days to come' (vs 27–28). Again in verse 29 he says, 'The revealer of mysteries showed you what is going to happen.'

Daniel's approach gives us some helpful hints on how to witness to non-Christians. First, he used a natural setting for talking about God. It is not easy to introduce the topic of God and to talk about him with people who have shown no interest in such a conversation. While it was *not necessary* for Daniel to talk about God in this conversation with the king, it was *possible* to do so. He pounced upon that opportunity.

We encounter many situations with people that lend themselves to turning the topic to spiritual things.

Wilberforce even *created* situations that made it possible to talk about Christ. Similarly we can use a topic people are thinking about and use that topic as a starting point for sharing the gospel.

Some time ago, youth unrest was a very big issue in Sri Lanka. The youth were revolting because they were disillusioned with the current generation of national leaders. I found that when I spoke with them about the issue of leadership, I could explain why Jesus was such a practical and exemplary leader. The opportunities were there — if I chose to use them. I confess that sometimes I did not take the crucial step of connecting the conversation with the topic of Christ. I was afraid of the reaction I would get. That was a totally unwarranted and sinful fear.

Second, Daniel told the king that God was responsible for everything Nebuchadnezzar had. When people notice something about us they like, we can use that as an opportunity to talk about God.

In his very helpful book on personal witness, *Good News Is for Sharing*, Leighton Ford tells how some Christians from an Eastern European country shared their faith when their country was under the grip of communism. They worked extremely hard at their jobs. 'We are not allowed to initiate a conversation about Jesus Christ in our country,' they said. 'But we can work hard and show that we are motivated people by our disciplined lives. When we are asked why, then we can explain it is because Jesus Christ is in us.'[2]

Witnessing for Christ is one of our primary responsibilities wherever we are. Wherever we go, we go as representatives of Christ to tell people what he has done for us. We go to our homes, to our workplaces, to the playing field, to our neighbourhoods, or wherever else we may go, saying, 'I am a witness for Christ in this place.'

In the diocese of Dornakal in South India, many Hindus turned to Christ when Bishop Vedanayagam Samuel Azariah served there. Bishop Azariah used to invite the newly baptised to place their hand on their head and say after him: 'I am a baptised Christian; woe is unto me if I preach not the gospel!'[3]

This commitment to witness was well expressed in the life of a poor village tailor in India named Punlik John. He had wanted to be a preacher, but he had to drop out of school because he failed his sixth-grade exams. A missionary, David Seamands (who later became well known for his books on emotional healing), helped him to decide to serve God as a lay person.

He set up his business in a poor village and darned people's torn clothes and stitched new clothes. When people came to him, he talked to them about Christ. Within a few months there was a small group ready for baptism. Then he went to Dr Seamands, handed these converts over to him, and moved to the next village. It is said that over six hundred people were baptised through the witness of this one man.

Focusing on God and on the needs of others
(2:25–30)

Daniel focused on God and on King Nebuchadnezzar's need rather than on himself. When King Nebuchadnezzar asked him, 'Are you able to tell me what I saw in my dream and interpret it?' (v 26), he could have said 'Yes' and taken the credit. That is what Arioch, the commander of the king's guard, did when he brought Daniel to the king. He said, 'I have found a man among the exiles of Judah who can tell the king what his dream means' (v 25). That was not quite true. Arioch did not find Daniel; Daniel went to him.

Daniel, on the other hand, immediately takes the attention away from himself and focuses it on God. He says, 'No wise man, enchanter, magician or diviner can explain to the king the mystery he has asked about, but there is a God in heaven who reveals mysteries. He has shown King Nebuchadnezzar what will happen in days to come' (vs 27–28). Again he says, 'As for me, this mystery was revealed to me, not because I have greater wisdom than other living men, but so that you, O king, may know the interpretation and that you may understand what went through your mind' (v 30). Daniel directly deflects any glory that might have come to him and instead focuses on the welfare of the king.

A threefold desire emerges from Daniel's introductory statements: a desire to honour God, a desire to deflect any glory that would come to himself, and a desire for the welfare of the king. Here are three motives of an effective witness. Paul expresses this threefold desire in 2 Corinthians 4:5: 'For we do not preach ourselves, but Jesus Christ as Lord, and ourselves as your servants for Jesus' sake.'

In recent years, some critics have associated evangelism with arrogance. This is a false accusation, for biblical evangelism at its heart is incompatible with arrogance.[4] But some Christians may have given room for this accusation because they have claimed they are better than other people rather than focusing on what a wonderful Saviour Jesus is.

William Wilberforce reflected a different attitude. On the night the vote to abolish the Slave Trade Act was taken in parliament, speaker after speaker rose to praise Wilberforce for his long and bruising battle against slavery. 'The House rose almost to a man and turned towards Wilberforce in a burst of Parliamentary cheers. Suddenly, above the roar of "hear, hear," and quite out of order, three hurrahs echoed and echoed while he sat, head bowed, tears streaming down his face.'[5] The house voted overwhelmingly for abolition.

How did Wilberforce celebrate the victory? We are told that he marked the passing of the bill by meditating on Psalm 115:1: 'Not to us, O LORD, not to us but to your name be the glory, because of your love and faithfulness.'[6] He replied to the Prime Minister's congratulatory note saying, 'You do me far more honour than I deserve. I am only one among many fellow labourers, and it is no more than justice to yourself to say, that to yourself and to the tone you have taken and the exertions you have made, our success is mainly to be attributed.'[7]

How sad it is to meet Christians who always talk about themselves and what they have done. And how refreshing to meet those who are so eager for God's glory that they don't spend much time dwelling on their achievements.

Introducing non-Christians to God (2:28–29, 37, 44–45)

We learn another lesson about witness by looking at the way Daniel introduced King Nebuchadnezzar to God. In verse 28 he says, 'There is a God in heaven who reveals mysteries.' In verse 29 he again presents him as 'the revealer of mysteries.' When we talk to someone who does not know much about God, or who has a concept of the divine that is very different from ours, we need to explain something about who this God is. That is what Daniel does here. It is not enough for us simply to say, 'God loves you.'

We face this challenge all the time in Sri Lanka as we speak to Buddhists and Hindus. Now even in the so-called post-Christian West people have various unbiblical views of the divine derived from humanistic, New Age, and Eastern religious sources.

Daniel says two things about God. First, he introduces him as 'a God in heaven'. Alan Millard points out that this 'gently leads the king to the thought of a being different from his own gods.'[8] As he is in heaven, he is not made by hands like Nebuchadnezzar's idols. In verse 37 Daniel tells Nebuchadnezzar, 'The God of heaven has given you dominion and power and might and glory.' In verse 44 he says, 'The God of heaven will set up a kingdom that will never be destroyed.' Then in verse 45 he calls God 'the great God.' In all these instances, God is presented as the supreme God. The reference to heaven and to God's might suggest that Daniel is pointing to the supremacy of God. Paul did this when preaching in Lystra and Athens, when he presented God as the Creator of the universe, which was another way of saying he is supreme (Acts 14:15; 17:25).

It is wise to introduce God as the supreme God to non-Christians. By simple logic, they can infer that if this God is indeed the supreme God, then it would be advisable to follow him. Later, when interpreting the dream, Daniel drives this point home clearly.

Second, Daniel introduces God as the One who reveals mysteries. Daniel follows the proven evangelistic strategy of showing God as someone who meets people's felt needs.

Nebuchadnezzar acknowledged a need for understanding a mystery. Daniel said God reveals those mysteries. The astrologers had told the king, 'No one can reveal [the dream] to the king except the gods, and they do not live among men.' Daniel presented to Nebuchadnezzar a God who can communicate with people.

Christians say, 'Jesus is the answer.' Others hear this and say, 'He is the answer to the questions Christians ask, not to our questions.' We must show them that Jesus does answer their questions; that he is, in fact, the only adequate answer to their questions.

The people of Athens had a shrine for an unknown God. They were concerned about not overlooking and perhaps offending a particular deity.[9] When preaching to them, Paul presented God as the One who would answer their yearning for security that stood behind that shrine (Acts 17:23).

In Sri Lanka we saw some wealthy and influential Buddhists take an interest in the gospel. Some accepted the Christian gospel. Most of them made contact with the gospel through a Christian friend. He knew of a need they had and told them that Christ could meet that need. We sometimes think this method works only with the poor and needy. But it is relevant to all people, for all people have needs. The challenge to us is to get close enough to know what people's needs are.

Confronting the arrogant with God's sovereignty (2:31–45)

We will not go into a detailed study of Nebuchadnezzar's dream and its interpretation. Briefly, it is about an awesome statue whose different parts represent four kingdoms. The head of gold is Nebuchadnezzar's kingdom. The chest and the arms of silver represent a kingdom to follow the Babylonian kingdom. The next kingdom is depicted by a belly and thighs made of bronze. The fourth kingdom is represented by legs of iron and feet made partly of iron and partly of clay.

There is no general agreement about which historical

kingdoms and periods of history are represented by each of these segments of the statue, and that is beyond the scope of this book. Besides, as a recent encyclopedia article on Daniel puts it, 'To focus too much attention on identifying the four kingdoms can result in failure to see the chapter's key feature.'[10] That key feature is a rock that strikes the statue and smashes it completely. The rock, in turn, becomes a huge mountain and fills the whole earth (vs 34–35). Daniel identifies the rock as the kingdom the God of heaven will set up that 'will never be destroyed' (v 44). Christians, of course, see this as Jesus Christ's kingdom.

Clearly the message God wants to get through to Nebuchadnezzar is that the Lord is sovereign over history and will ultimately set up an eternal kingdom. The message of God's sovereignty is given in at least three ways. First, God is identified as the God of heaven three times in Daniel's discourse (vs 28, 37, 44). Second, after acknowledging that Nebuchadnezzar is 'the king of kings', Daniel tells him, 'The God of heaven has given you dominion and power and might and glory; in your hands he has placed mankind.' Nebuchadnezzar would have claimed that he earned all his glory by his own power. But Daniel has the nerve to tell him that it was all given to him by God! Third, Daniel tells Nebuchadnezzar his kingdom will not last forever, whereas God's kingdom will (vs 39, 44).

In this last chapter of this book we will see how the message of God's sovereignty encourages the faithful who are baffled by the growth of evil in the world. But God's sovereignty can also be a strong message for powerful and arrogant unbelievers like Nebuchadnezzar.

Working with 'power converts' (2:46–47)

What a surprising reaction to Daniel's discourse we see from Nebuchadnezzar:

> Then King Nebuchadnezzar fell prostrate before Daniel and paid him honour and ordered that an offering and incense be presented to him. The king said to Daniel, 'Surely your God is

the God of gods and the Lord of kings and a revealer of mysteries, for you were able to reveal this mystery' (vs 46–47).

This brutal despot's attitude changes drastically. He accepts a message that undermines his authority, and he worships the messenger who is an exile from a third-rate country! Then he even accepts the supremacy of the God of this third-rate country.

Has he been converted? By Daniel 3 he is back to his paganism and his old brutality. He has had a religious experience and has seen the power of God. Such an 'experience can stimulate an impressive response at a superficial level and leave us untouched in the depths of our being.'[11]

There's a warning to us here about proclaiming that someone has been converted because of a statement he or she makes after experiencing God's power. Someone has called these people 'power Christians' — people who respond to the power of God but not to the core of the gospel of Jesus Christ, which presents God as being Holy-Love in addition to being powerful.

Yet such an experience could be a first step toward conversion. A demonstration of God's power could grab the attention of a disinterested nonbeliever and open the door for presenting the gospel. In Daniel 4 Nebuchadnezzar expresses what seems to be the fruit of genuine conversion. This experience of having his dream explained would surely have been a first step toward his conversion.

Remembering our humble beginnings (2:46–49)

It is surprising to see Nebuchadnezzar fall prostrate before Daniel and order that an offering and incense be presented to him (v 46). It is even more surprising to find no protest about this from the usually modest and religiously orthodox Daniel. This is a strong point in favour of the authenticity of this story. One would not include something like this in a fictional tract aimed at encouraging religious fidelity at a time of religious desolation under foreign powers. Many critics today view the book of Daniel as a tract of this type.[12]

Did Daniel accept this homage? We do not know. Perhaps this is an occasion when he failed God in not protesting about what was happening. The Scriptures often record heroes doing the wrong thing. Even today, committed Christians in public life, being as vulnerable as they are, make mistakes.

Nebuchadnezzar did not stop with an offering; he gave more gifts and honours that Daniel could legitimately accept. 'Then the king placed Daniel in a high position and lavished many gifts on him. He made him ruler over the entire province of Babylon and placed him in charge of all its wise men' (v 48).

So Daniel prospered. But in his prosperity he did not forget his friends. He was a person from a despised minority community who had climbed to the top of the social ladder. Often such people are so desirous of being fully accepted by the social elite that they forget their roots and avoid their own people. Not Daniel. The chapter ends by saying, 'Moreover, at Daniel's request the king appointed Shadrach, Meshach and Abednego administrators over the province of Babylon, while Daniel himself remained at the royal court' (v 49).

STUDY QUESTIONS

2:24–30   How does attempting to witness help you maintain your commitment in non-Christian surroundings?

Give examples of how various situations you face could be used as opportunities to witness for Christ.

2:25–30   Why is it so difficult in today's society to deflect glory from ourselves to God?

What can we do to make sure that we are not taking for ourselves any glory that belongs to God?

2:28–29, 37, 44–45   What unbiblical views about God do you encounter today? How can you introduce the God of the Bible to people with such views?

What are some of the felt needs of people you seek to witness to today?

2:31–45   How would the message of God's sovereignty over circumstances and over history help you when witnessing to people?

2:46–49   In contrast to Daniel, Christians often try to hide their humble beginnings. What are the dangers of this attitude?

6

Commitment:
the Key to Heroism

Daniel 3:1–18

In 1837 three young Methodist ministers, James Calvert, John Hunt, Thomas Jaggar, and their wives set out from England for the Fiji Islands. Theirs was a difficult assignment. The work there was only three years old, and the people were still cannibals. Hardly any fruit was seen during their first few years of service. Then in 1845 revival swept through the Islands. Chief Thakombau, who had been the main opponent of Christianity, was converted. Within a few years a complete transformation of the islands had taken place as the gospel took hold of the people there.[1]

The captain of the ship that took the three English couples from England tried to persuade them to change their mind about going to the islands. He told Calvert, 'You will lose your lives and the lives of those with you if you go among such savages.' Calvert replied, 'We died before we came here.'[2]

In the previous century the founder of their movement, John Wesley, had said, 'Give me a hundred men who love God with all their hearts and fear nothing but sin, and I will move the world.' Those three young missionaries were part of God's answer to Wesley's prayer. His words also summarise the heart of commitment. Loving God and fearing sin are the keys to an effective Christian life for anyone who wants to be obedient in this fallen world. We see this type of commitment in Daniel's friends in chapter 3.

When we must disobey our benefactors (3:1–12)

The chapter begins with the report: 'King Nebuchadnezzar made an image of gold, ninety feet high and nine feet wide, and set it up on the plain of Dura in the province of Babylon' (v 1). We are not told who was portrayed by this enormous statue. It was probably not Nebuchadnezzar. Historians have not found evidence of Babylonian kings being worshipped by their subjects. Gleason Archer says that it may have been a statue of Nebuchadnezzar's patron god Nabu (or Nebo). If so, bowing down to the statue would be equivalent to taking a pledge of allegiance to his viceroy, Nebuchadnezzar.

The top officials from all over Babylon were summoned for the dedication (vs 2–3). A herald instructed everyone present to 'fall down and worship the image of gold' as soon as they heard the sound of different musical instruments (vs 4–5). And then he warned, 'Whoever does not fall down and worship will immediately be thrown into a blazing furnace' (v 6).

As soon as they heard the sound of the instruments 'all the peoples... fell down and worshipped the image' (vs 7–8). Well, not exactly all the people — Shadrach, Meshach and Abednego did not bow down and worship the image. Nothing is said about Daniel. He may have succeeded in keeping away from the event. Or, because he was so high up in the administration and trusted so much by the king, no one may have dared to make a complaint against him.

The astrologers must have been jealous of these foreigners who had been promoted to such high positions by the king. They would have pounced on this opportunity to put them in their place. Verse 8 says, 'At this time some astrologers came forward and denounced the Jews.' They went to the king and reminded him of the decree he had issued about falling down and worshipping the image of gold and the consequences of not doing so (vs 9–11). Then they stated their complaint: 'But there are some Jews whom you have set over the affairs of the province of Babylon — Shadrach, Meshach and Abednego — who pay no attention to you, O king. They neither serve your gods nor worship the image of gold you have set up' (v 12).

They accused the three Jews of ingratitude and disloyalty. That is why they described them as 'some Jews whom *you have set* over the affairs of the province of Babylon.' It is like saying, 'You went out of your way to help these people and gave them jobs they didn't really deserve. Now see how ungrateful and defiant they are!'

It is very hard for us to go against a person who has helped us. But as Christians we sometimes have to do this and risk being misunderstood as ungrateful and dishonourable people, especially if our disobedience humiliates the one who helped us. Of course, we can be as polite and as respectful as possible in order to reduce the humiliation on our benefactor.

Sometimes our benefactors are our own parents. They may want us to follow a certain profession, so they help us in our studies at much personal cost to themselves. Then we say that, because of the call of God, we are going into a profession that is not very rewarding financially, like elementary teaching or student ministry. It could appear as if their sacrificial support has been misused by an ungrateful child.

I have seen some children who have done this, but who, despite their meagre resources, were model children to their parents in their old age. Then, many years after the initial hurt, those parents were very proud of and grateful to their unselfish children. But in the early years they resented their choice of career.

When it is time to obey, not talk (3:13–16)

'Furious with rage, Nebuchadnezzar summoned Shadrach, Meshach and Abednego. So these men were brought before the king' (v 13). He asks them whether what has been said is true (v 14), and then he gives them a chance to disprove their accusers by going through the music ritual over again. Possibly he did not trust the astrologers who brought the complaint against Shadrach, Meshach and Abednego because he suspected that they were jealous of them. He may have wanted to give them another chance so that the humiliation brought to his name could be mended. Anyway, a wise king would not sentence three trusted officials to death simply on the basis of hearsay.

Nebuchadnezzar firmly tells them, 'But if you do not worship it, you will be thrown immediately into the blazing furnace. Then what god will be able to rescue you from my hand?' (v 15). What a challenge Shadrach, Meshach and Abednego faced! Robert Anderson makes the point that, 'It is one thing to defy a decree in the relative obscurity of the gathered multitude; it is quite another to continue that defiance face to face with the personification of authority and the embodiment of power.'[3]

Their response is as brave as ever. They say, 'O King Nebuchadnezzar, we do not need to defend ourselves before you in this matter' (v 16). Then they go on to state their unwillingness to bow down whatever the consequences may be.

Why do they say there is no need for them to defend themselves? Nebuchadnezzar has said, 'What god will be able to rescue you from my hand?' He should have known better. He had already experienced the power of the God of Shadrach, Meshach and Abednego when Daniel explained the mystery of his dream. On that occasion he had called God 'the God of gods' (2:47). So Shadrach, Meshach and Abednego knew that it was not the time to introduce their God to him. There are times when we need to talk and discuss our convictions. But this was not one of those times. This was the time for action.

Nebuchadnezzar needed to know that God is not one who simply needs to be discussed; he needs to be followed! He is not just someone to go to when we have a problem, but someone to obey as our only Lord. This, then, was not the time to glorify God through words; it was a time to glorify God through obedience. It was the time for sacrifice.

I know people who keep discussing an issue that will involve costly obedience on their part and, by so doing, delay having to take the step of obedience.

I once hosted two 'Christians' from a neighbouring country who came to see me through an introduction by a mutual friend. From my conversation with them I gathered that they were involved in some unethical business deals. Our conversation moved into a discussion of Christians in business. They kept asking me questions like, 'As a Christian, can I lie once in a while? Must I tell the whole truth all the time, or can I withhold some information to my advantage?'

I found that I was getting very annoyed during this discussion. I realised that these two people were not serious about practising Christianity. They just wanted to discuss what the Christian view on ethical issues is. Later I thought that I should have asked them something like this: 'If I can convince you that Christians must be a hundred per cent honest all the time, will you be a hundred per cent honest?' I sensed that they were willing to discuss but not to obey the Christian way.

Some people keep talking about being unsure of God's plan for their lives. They say they are waiting for a clear call from God. George Verwer, the founder of Operation Mobilization, a movement that has mobilised thousands of young people in the work of evangelism, once said, 'Some people say they are waiting for a call. What they need is a kick in the pants!'

We must be willing to die (3:17–18)

Nebuchadnezzar placed a challenge before Shadrach, Meshach and Abednego. He said, 'If you do not worship [the image], you will be thrown immediately into a blazing furnace. Then what god will be able to rescue you from my hand?' (v 15). How weak they must have looked at that moment — three young foreigners, seemingly forsaken by God, facing the wrath of a powerful ruler.

There are times when evil seems to hold sway and control all that happens. It wasn't for nothing that Paul called

Satan 'the god of this age' (2 Cor 4:4). We, too, will face situations in our places of work, our neighbourhoods, or in our places of witness when we feel weak and helpless as hostile forces close in on us.

The three friends may have been tempted to compromise just this one time. Then they could have continued to live and to have a great influence for God in a dark age. What good could they do for God if they were dead? Was it not God's blessing to bring them to the top? Surely after God had caused them to climb so miraculously to the top, he would not expect them to throw away this great opportunity to have an influence for good.

Because they wanted to be obedient to God, Shadrach, Meshach and Abednego were willing to give up all that they had achieved. Listen to what they said: 'If we are thrown into the blazing furnace, the God we serve is able to save us from it, and he will rescue us from your hand, O king. But even if he does not, we want you to know, O king, that we will not serve your gods or worship the image of gold you have set up' (vs 17–18). Can you see their trust in the sovereignty of God? He *can* save them. But that may not be his will. If so, they are willing to die.

George Mueller (1805–1898) was a man who achieved an extraordinary amount of good for the kingdom during his lifetime. His orphanages provided homes for thousands of homeless children and also supplied the church with many effective Christian workers. After retiring from the orphanages when he was seventy years old, he launched an itinerant evangelistic ministry that lasted nearly seventeen years. He visited forty-two countries, travelling over two hundred thousand miles and preaching to three million hearers. And this was before the time of aeroplanes and loudspeakers! Someone once asked him the secret of his service for God. He replied:

> There was a day when I died, utterly died: died to George Mueller, his opinions, preferences, tastes and will — died to the world, its approval or censure, died to the approval or blame even of my brethren and friends — and since then I have studied only to show myself approved unto God.[4]

Each of us will face the challenge of death to self in different ways. It may not take the form of a definite crisis. In fact, there is a sense in which we crucify self daily. The thing that is common to all is the challenge of being willing to say, 'Not my will, but yours.'

Not all Christians are willing to pay that price. The cost seems to be too great. They want what the world has to offer, and they want it 'now'.

One of the saddest things I have encountered in youth ministry has been to see young people who are full of enthusiasm for the work of God drop out suddenly when the will of God clashes with their own will. They work hard at youth ministry, they are orthodox in their beliefs, and everything seems to go fine until the path of obedience takes them away from what they want to do. Then they wilt, choosing their will rather than God's.

Often it happens over marrying a spiritually incompatible person. They know they are going against the clear teaching of Scripture, but they *have to* have this person they have fallen in love with. Sometimes it is a question of revenge. Someone has humiliated them, and they *have to* get even, though that means disobeying God's command to love our enemies. With deep sorrow I have to conclude that they may be doing ministry because they like it, not primarily because it is God's will for them.

The need for heroes

Christian writers bemoan the fact that there are too few heroes today for our youth to emulate.[5] They know that each generation needs models of total commitment to God.

Yet many of us prefer to admire our heroes from a distance. Some parents teach their children the exciting stories about heroes like Amy Carmichael, Hudson Taylor and Dr Ida Scudder, but strongly oppose these same children when later in life they want to follow their example.

Few people today are willing to pay the price of heroism. True heroes are rarely admired when they are doing their heroic work. Usually they are regarded as fools, fanatics, and unbalanced people, who have taken their work far too seriously.

One of the most influential theologians of our time, Carl Henry, has this to say about the path of obedience:

> To an unregenerate world, not only will Jesus seem out of step with reality, but so will his disciples. Think and act like the world and the world will embrace us, for then being a Christian doesn't make a speck of difference. But truly live in the Spirit world as did early Christians and worldlings will consider us zombies — over the brink and stark mad.[6]

Let's apply this principle to a situation you might face in the workplace. Your boss asks you to say something slanderous about a colleague. He promises to 'look after you' if you comply. But the slandered person will lose his job. If you don't comply, you too might lose your job. That would be 'death' to you. After years of faithful service, why should you lose your job because of the unreasonableness of your boss? Besides, you have a family to look after. It would seem selfish to let them suffer because of your principles. Yet believing the sovereignty of God, you choose the way of death and refuse to obey your boss' request to slander your coworker.

That is heroism: the willingness to be true to our principles whatever the cost may be. We must be willing to lose all the earthly treasure and honour we have earned through hard work, if that is the price of obedience.

I heard of a Vietnamese pastor who made a long journey on foot from his village to what was then known as Saigon as the Vietnam War was coming to a close. Like many other Christians, he was coming to Saigon seeking a chance to leave Vietnam for security in a Western country. I do not think that this was wrong. But, as he came near to Saigon, he realised that for him the call of God was to remain with his people. So he turned and went back to his village, to the prospects of danger, hunger, loneliness, and even death. He was willing to die and, despite all that he could have done if he was alive, he did not think going back was a waste. He knew that when God calls us to die, he is opening the door to real life.

The gateway to life

To die doing the will of God is, in the final reckoning, the gateway to life. I do not know whether Shadrach, Meshach and Abednego knew that, but we know it. Jesus said, 'For whoever wants to save his life will lose it, but whoever loses his life for me and for the gospel will save it' (Mk 8:35).

That is why total commitment is no great achievement on our part. Because God is sovereign, when we make what seems like a big sacrifice, it is no sacrifice at all. We can willingly give up everything we have gained for the sake of obedience to God, knowing that life and victory await us in the end.

Death opens the way for the excitement of being carried along in the victorious stream of God's sovereignty. When we die, we say that what is important is not our will but God's will. But we know that God's will is best. When our will clashes with God's will, we choose God's will because that is the best choice in every way. In the final analysis, the way of death is the pathway to the deepest and the fullest enjoyment!

David Livingstone (1813–1873) was a Scottish missionary and explorer who gave up much in terms of earthly treasure to follow the call of God. He renounced a medical career in Scotland in order to go to the interior of Africa. His work opened up that country for missionary activity and for trade that broke the stranglehold slave traders had on the people.

'He was attacked and maimed by a lion, his home was destroyed during the Boer War, his body was often racked by fever and dysentery, and his wife died on the field.'[7] Someone once told him, 'Dr Livingstone, you must have sacrificed a lot for the gospel.' His response was: 'Sacrifice? The only sacrifice is to live outside the will of God.'

STUDY QUESTIONS

3:1–12 Have you ever had to displease someone you were indebted to because of the call of God? How did that person respond to your action?

3:13–16 Have you encountered people who seemed to be evading the step of commitment? How did you respond to them?

    In what situations have you felt weak and helpless when hostile forces seemed very powerful? What helped you at such times?

3:17–18 Though death to self is a daily experience for Christians, many (like George Mueller) have had a specific crisis experience that sealed the issue of commitment for them. What has been your experience? Is this the time of commitment for you?

    In what areas is your commitment to God tested today? How might following the way of the cross be dangerous to your welfare? How do your Christian principles make you the 'odd person out'?

    How would a Christian hero or heroine act today? What specific actions and attitudes would make that person's behaviour heroic?

    Do you remember specific instances where by dying to self (losing your life) you found life? Explain.

CHAPTER

7

God Is with Us

Daniel 3:19–30

In the previous chapter we listed some of the sacrifices David Livingstone made as he obeyed God's call to Africa. How could he endure that hardship over such an extended period of time?

Someone asked him that very question. He replied that the words of Jesus kept ringing in his ear, 'Lo, I am with you alway, even unto the end of the world' (Mt 28:20, KJV). He once said, 'Without Christ, not one step; with him, anywhere.' The presence of Christ made the difference. That made the pain of separation from loved ones, physical sickness, and all the other trials he faced bearable.

Shadrach, Meshach and Abednego also made the wonderful discovery of God's presence while they were in the flames. But before that they had to face an angry king!

Heroism is often unappreciated (3:19–23)

The three men had just made a heroic statement about their willingness to die for their principles (3:16–18). But the king, true to form, had no appreciation for their commitment. Verses 19 and 20 says, 'Then Nebuchadnezzar was furious with Shadrach, Meshach and Abednego, and his attitude toward them changed. He ordered the furnace heated seven times hotter than usual and commanded some of the strongest soldiers in the army to tie up Shadrach, Meshach and Abednego and throw them into the blazing furnace.'

Nebuchadnezzar feels humiliated and that his authority is being challenged. This is not the first time that obedience to God is seen as defiance of man. In a world opposed to God's ways, those who obey him fully will often be accused of treachery. That was how those in authority responded to Jesus. And he told his followers: '"No servant is greater than his master." If they persecuted me, they will persecute you also' (Jn 15:20). So some of our greatest acts of obedience to God will earn us punishment and rejection on earth.

Nebuchadnezzar asks that the furnace be heated seven times hotter than usual. Gleason Archer explains that additional bellows would have been inserted under the blazing coals. The strongest soldiers are employed to put the men into the furnace. 'So these men, wearing their robes, trousers, turbans and other clothes, were bound and thrown into the blazing furnace' (v 21). The furnace was 'so hot that the flames of the fire killed the soldiers who took up Shadrach, Meshach and Abednego' (v 22). Verse 23 sounds like the conclusion of a heroic story: 'And these three men, firmly tied, fell into the blazing furnace.'

The excitement of God's deliverance (3:24–25)

But it was not the end. Verse 24 begins a new and exciting phase of the story: 'Then King Nebuchadnezzar leaped to his feet in amazement and asked his advisers, "Weren't there three men that we tied up and threw into the fire?" They replied, "Certainly, O king"' (v 24). Nebuchadnezzar is standing face to face with a miracle. 'He said, "Look! I see four men walking around in the fire, unbound and unharmed, and the fourth looks like a son of the gods"' (v 25). In fact, two miracles have taken place: the three people are unharmed, and there is a fourth person 'like a son of the gods'.

We cannot be sure about the identity of this fourth person. The old King James Version translation, 'like the Son of God', led many to believe that this was a preincarnate appearance of Christ. But that is not a correct translation. Besides, the pagan King Nebuchadnezzar would not know enough to be able to identify the Son of God.

Though we cannot say who the fourth person was, we can be sure that Nebuchadnezzar saw someone who looked like a divine being. Whoever that person was, whether it was God or Jesus or an angel or some other heavenly being, God expressed his solidarity with his three faithful servants.

God had promised in Isaiah 43:2–3, 'When you pass through the waters, I will be with you.... When you walk through the fire, you will not be burned; the flames will not set you ablaze. For I am the LORD, your God, the Holy One of Israel, your Saviour.' Now his promise is fulfilled literally.

It is interesting to note that Shadrach, Meshach and Abednego did not escape the flames. They experienced this wonderful deliverance only after they had fearlessly expressed their commitment to God and had gone right into the flames because of it.[1]

Some Christians have no recent testimony of God's deliverance in their lives. Their Christian experience is devoid of freshness, and life is a bore. Often Christians get that way when they do not launch out in costly obedience to God. They may not commit any big sins. But they avoid the fire. By 'keeping out of trouble', they fail to give God an opportunity to show his mighty deliverance.

When we launch out in obedience to God, we can be sure of a life with danger, inconvenience, and suffering. Paul said, 'In fact, everyone who wants to live a godly life in Christ Jesus will be persecuted' (2 Tim 3:12). But we can also be sure that we will not suffer from boredom! Our problems become means to God's deliverances, and that makes life meaningful and exciting.

Our job is a danger-filled joy. We go to battle for God's kingdom and fight against evil. We are bruised, but we also experience God's healing touch. We are brought to situations of great need, but those open the floodgates of God's provision. We are rejected by people, but that opens the door to God's nearness and comfort.

God is with us (3:25)

God has special ways of ministering to our needs and assuring us that he is with us in our hour of crisis. I think that is one way 'the Spirit himself testifies with our spirit that we are God's children' (Rom 8:16). This message of assurance from the Spirit comes to us in different ways. But however it comes, God wants us to know that he is with us and is supporting us.

That assurance may come through the passage you read for your devotions which, you find, speaks directly to your present situation. You are thrilled when you realise that the sovereign God knows you will go through this problem and arranged for you to read this passage the day you most need its message. The assurance of God's presence may come through a letter or a kind word from someone that speaks to your situation. It may come in the form of a cheque in the post when you are in desperate financial need. The timing, the appropriateness to your situation, the way it ministers to your need, all bear the stamp of 'the comfort of the Lord'.

When you realise that the sovereign God cares enough to minister to you in this special way, you have courage to go on, you have a joy that helps you face the pain, and you think to yourself, 'This is no sacrifice. God is with me! I wouldn't exchange this for anything in the world.'

'God is with me.' You may *seem* to be all alone. Perhaps there is no one in your place of work or family who is a committed Christian. Others may not understand you or appreciate what you are trying to do. They may even oppose you. But Jesus is with you. And that makes all the difference.

I had a strange experience some years ago when I attended a board meeting of a Christian organisation in a foreign land. As far as I remember, I was the only person from the so-called Third World at that meeting. I think I was also the youngest person at the meeting and the only one whose ticket had been paid for by the organisation. The others paid their own way. I was among Christians, but I felt like a stranger.

To add to my embarrassment, I found I was the only one at the meeting who was uneasy about a huge ministry project this organisation was going to initiate in a Third World country. The funds were available, but I felt that in terms of the total impact on the church in that land, the disadvantages of the project outweighed the benefits. The donor was present at the meeting. But I kept registering my opposition to the project. I think some of the people were perplexed by the actions of this young rebel from the Third World.

I do not enjoy confrontation, and I felt very lonely at that meeting. When we broke for coffee or for meals, I would rush up to my room, fall on my knees and talk to God. I knew that at least God would understand what I was trying to say. That gave me strength.

There is a simple song that has been an inspiration to me over the years, and its message may inspire you to take the path of costly obedience to God. Its first verse and chorus go like this:

> It may be in the valley, where countless dangers hide;
> It may be in the sunshine that I, in peace, abide;
> But this one thing I know — if it be dark or fair;
> If Jesus goes with me, I'll go anywhere.

> If Jesus goes with me, I'll go
> Anywhere!
> 'Tis heaven to me, where'er I may be,
> If he is there!
> I count it a privilege here his cross to bear;
> If Jesus goes with me, I'll go
> Anywhere.[2]

How total commitment challenges the world
(3:26–30)

After what he saw, Nebuchadnezzar's attitude changed completely. He 'approached the opening of the blazing furnace and shouted, "Shadrach, Meshach and Abednego, servants of the Most High God, come out! Come here!"' (v 26). He calls the God of the Jews the Most High God! Just after dedicating a statue of his own god, he declares that the God of the Jews is the Supreme God.

How did he come to such a conclusion about God? He gives his reason when he speaks next. The three young men have, in the meantime, come out of the furnace, and the people have seen that they have not been harmed (v 27). Nebuchadnezzar says, 'Praise be to the God of Shadrach, Meshach and Abednego, who has sent his angel and rescued his servants!' (v 28). Then he mentions what really impressed him: 'They trusted in him and defied the king's command and were willing to give up their lives rather than serve or worship any god except their own God' (v 28).

The persecutor sees the commitment of the persecuted and connects it with a miracle performed by God. The combination of miracle and commitment drives him to praise God for inspiring such commitment in the lives of his followers.

People are often not willing to listen to what we say. But they cannot help observing how we live. If they see in us the type of commitment that makes us willing to sacrifice our very lives for the sake of our God, they will be challenged by our commitment.

Such people usually live for themselves and compromise their principles to get what they want. But after they have what they were looking for, they realise that they are still dissatisfied and unfulfilled. Yet, blinded as they are by the lure of earthly pleasure, they keep pursuing this elusive bubble called satisfaction by using sinful methods. They may look at us and laugh at how much we are missing because of our religiousness. But one day they will come to their senses and realise that we have the satisfaction they have looked for but never found.

They see us forego promotions in our place of work. They see us give the little we have to help the needy. They see us face ridicule and persecution and note that in the midst of all this we seem to be happy and contented. They conclude that this Master Jesus, whom we follow, must indeed be very precious to us. A thirst comes to them to know the satisfaction we know, to commit themselves to a cause that is capable of really exciting its followers.

When people get disillusioned with materialism and its broken promises and look elsewhere for meaning to life, what will they see when they look at the church? Will they see Christians caught up in the same rat race as the rest of society? Will they see us refusing to help others, because we are so wrapped up in ourselves? Will they see us putting others down as we climb to the top? Will they see us committing the same sins they see in the society: sexual immorality, greed, and the desire to put up a show of success? Will they see our churches so intent on attracting people with entertainment that we have stopped challenging them to moral purity? Will they see churches, in their craving to grow, causing hurt to other churches, just like in the competitive marketplace they are trying to escape from?

If that is what they see, they will look elsewhere for an answer to their emptiness. Could this be one reason why Eastern religions are growing in the West? In Sri Lanka the Buddhists are spending large sums of money to send missionaries to Western countries because they feel Buddhism is the answer to the moral indiscipline they see in 'Christian' countries.

A young theology professor, Carl F. H. Henry, wrote a book called *The Uneasy Conscience of Modern Fundamentalism*, which he later described as 'a tract for the times'.[3] The editor of *Decision* magazine, Sherwood Wirt, said: 'The book dropped like a bomb into the peaceful summer Bible conference atmosphere of the post-war evangelical community.[4] It pointed out many of the shortcomings of the evangelical movement and is credited to have done much to challenge the evangelicals of that time to take the call to social concerns more seriously. In this book, Henry challenged, "We must confront the world *now* with an ethic to make it tremble and with a dynamic to give it hope."[5]

That is still our call today. Let us pray that when the world looks at us it will be captivated by Jesus and fascinated by what he can do in a person's life. Let us pray that our commitment to Christ's principles of justice, love, and holiness will make the Christian way stand out as the answer to the ills of the world. And it is! But the world must see it to believe it.

F. W. Boreham, a popular preacher of an earlier generation, tells the story of a boy from the South Sea islands who was in a school where the missionary bishop, John Selwyn, taught. The boy had come from a barbarous society, and one day the bishop had to rebuke him sternly for his behaviour. 'The boy instantly flew into a passion and struck the bishop a cruel blow in the face. The bishop said nothing, but turned and walked quietly away.' The boy's behaviour went from bad to worse, until he had to be returned to his own island as incorrigible. There he soon lapsed into all the debasements of the people among whom he lived.

Many years later, a missionary in that island was summoned to visit a sick man. It was Bishop Selwyn's old student. He was dying and wanted to be baptised as a Christian. After the preparation was done and he was baptised, the missionary asked him whether he wanted to take a new name to mark his conversion. 'Call me John Selwyn,' the dying man replied, 'because he taught me what Christ was like that day when I struck him.'[6]

We long for the day when more and more of those who are angry with what we stand for will bow their knee to Christ because they cannot shake off from their minds the memory of our radiant testimony.

That is what happened to Nebuchadnezzar. He was so impressed by what he saw that he even gave legal protection to the God of Shadrach, Meshach and Abednego — something God really does not need! He said, 'Therefore I decree that people of any nation or language who say anything against the God of Shadrach, Meshach and Abednego be cut into pieces and their houses be turned into piles of rubble, for no other god can save in this way' (v 29).

The three friends also went up in the Babylonian hierarchy: 'Then the king promoted Shadrach, Meshach and Abednego in the province of Babylon' (v 30). Such a promotion is something we cannot be sure of today. Obedience to God sometimes takes us down, not up, in earthly kingdoms. But in the kingdom of God, which is where progress really matters from the perspective of eternity, obedience always takes us higher — higher in experiencing the joy of the Lord and higher in yielding fruit that lasts. Yet earthly promotions do open doors for us to have a wider influence for good. Because this can bring new opportunities for service to the kingdom, we accept them as blessings from God.

STUDY QUESTIONS

3:19–23   Can you think of heroic deeds done in today's world that met with anger from other people? Explain.

3:24–25   How has God expressed his solidarity with you when you were facing a crisis? When has he, by some unexpected providence, shown you that he is with you?

Was it after you took a costly step of obedience that you experienced, in a special way, the nearness and deliverance of God? Explain.

Has the Christian life become unexciting to you because you have not launched out into the 'second mile' of service and obedience? What can you do to change this state of affairs?

3:25   What should you do in a crisis to ensure that you experience the nearness of God and overcome the temptation to panic and become bitter?

3:26–30   How must the church change if it is to challenge the world through its total commitment to Christ? What are some of the things we should do to cause these changes?

Do you know of people whose promotion in their career was directly linked to their costly commitment to Christian principles? Do you know of people who were not promoted as they should have been because of such commitment? Explain.

CHAPTER

8

Confronting the Powerful with God's Power

Daniel 4:1–18

The Youth for Christ ministry in Sri Lanka often has programmes for the parents of our youth, so that they may know who these people are that are influencing their children. I speak at many of these programmes, and I usually give an evangelistic message. Some years ago I spoke at one of these meetings on God's love, using the parable of the Prodigal Son. After my talk, I asked the audience whether they had any questions. A businessman expressed to me that he was quite unimpressed with this parable and with what I had said. He said he did not need God like that son did. He had come to the top without God's help. Perhaps weak people needed this God, but not him!

I returned home wondering what type of message is appropriate for a person like that businessman. Many powerful and self-confident people take no notice of God and think they do not need religion. We talk to them about Christ, receive a condescending rejection, and we wonder, 'Will they ever respond to God?'

People must have thought the same thing about King Nebuchadnezzar. Yet Daniel 4, which is recorded as having been written by him, describes how he came to acknowledge God as his Lord. He begins and ends with praise to God, and in between tells the story of his conversion.

Some months after my encounter with the business-man, I was studying Daniel 4, and I felt it held a key to ministering to successful people like him.

No one is beyond the reach of God's love (4:1)

Nebuchadnezzar seemed an unlikely candidate for conversion. He was rich, powerful, wicked, and arrogant. We sometimes avoid witnessing to such people. Yet the Bible teaches that no one should be considered beyond the reach of God's love. Jesus said, 'Whoever comes to me I will never drive away' (Jn 6:37).

Daniel 4:1 follows 'the accepted style of ancient letter writing' where the author first 'names himself and those whom he is addressing.'[1] This is followed by a customary greeting: 'King Nebuchadnezzar, To the peoples, nations and men of every language, who live in all the world: May you prosper greatly!' (v 1).

If we addressed a document to such a wide audience, we would be regarded as megalomaniacs. But a king can command such a hearing. Scripture clearly implies that a king is not more important in God's sight than a poor unknown saint in an obscure village (see 1 Corinthians 12). But when a person of high influence in the world is converted, he or she can make an impact on a wide spectrum of people.

We should never declare anyone 'unconvertable' because he or she is high in society. When we follow Paul's injunction to pray for rulers (1 Tim 2:1,2), we should pray for their conversion also. If we get a chance to speak to them, we could try to use the opportunity to say a word for Jesus. We are reminded of Herod Agrippa's words to Paul, 'Do you think that in such a short time you can persuade me to be a Christian?' and Paul's reply, 'Short time or long — I pray God that not only you but all who are listening to me today may become what I am, except for these chains' (Acts 26:28–29).

The process from signs and wonders to conversion (4:2-3)

Verse 2 introduces the content of the letter: 'It is my pleasure to tell you about the miraculous signs and wonders that the Most High God has performed for me.' Then follows King Nebuchadnezzar's statement of praise to God: 'How great are his signs, how mighty his wonders! His kingdom is an eternal kingdom; his dominion endures from generation to generation' (v 3). He declares that God's kingdom is much more vast than his own and that it will last forever, unlike his own kingdom. This arrogant king has been humbled to see that, in God's sight, his greatness is nothing.

The king also mentions what caused his change of heart. Verse 2 says that it was 'the miraculous signs and wonders that the Most High God has performed for me.' Earlier we saw that when Daniel revealed and interpreted the king's dream, Nebuchadnezzar fell prostrate before Daniel and made an enthusiastic statement about God's power (2:46). But that did not make him a convert. Now we see that while it did not make him a convert, it started a process that resulted in what seems to have been a genuine conversion. In other words, the signs did what signs are supposed to do. They are supposed to point to something or someone. In this case they pointed to God, the originator of the signs.

It is often said that signs may be relevant when we minister to the poor and the illiterate, but they are of no value when we evangelise rich and sophisticated people. The Bible leaves no room for such a conclusion. God captured the attention of the highly educated. Moses through a miraculous burning bush and through two other miracles (Exod 3—4). In Paul's ministry, Sergius Paulus, the proconsul in Cyprus (Acts 13:12), and Publius, the chief official of Malta (Acts 28:7–10), were reached through miraculous signs. Here we see the powerful Nebuchadnezzar reached through signs and wonders.

Nebuchadnezzar also suffered from fear, like illiterate people do. Today sophisticated people may hide their fear, but we know they still feel it when there is a personal or family crisis. We can go to those people in their hour of need, pray for their needs to almighty God, and direct them to the Source of real security for their lives. We need not be reluctant to ask the Lord to reveal his power to those we seek to witness to, and we can take some steps in that direction, like praying for a sick person's healing.

There is a lot of controversy in the church today about what is called 'power evangelism'. Many Christians are afraid of some of the extremes they have seen in this ministry. Indeed there have been many extreme expressions recently in ministries emphasising signs and wonders. Too many things are being attributed to demons, sometimes even resulting in the down-playing of human responsibility for evil deeds. ('The Devil made me do it' is no longer just a joke!) Physical healing is often presented as God's will for every prayer for healing. Some leaders discourage the use of medicine and other sources of what is wrongly called 'natural healing'. (Actually, all healing is divine.)

The emphasis on God's power, in some instances, has resulted in a neglect of holiness and of careful study and teaching of 'the whole counsel of God'. Sometimes the 'power evangelist' has been put on a pedestal and permitted to abuse his power for personal gain. Too much attention is given to reports of miracles, which is giving birth to a generation of 'sign seekers' rather than 'Christ seekers'.

Anything taken to an extreme is wrong. But we must not let extremes cause us to avoid completely something that is clearly taught in Scripture. As in many things in life, the answer to misuse is not disuse. Misuse should motivate us to look for ways of proper use. The Bible does not make a 'big deal' about signs. But the early Christians looked for and prayed for opportunities to capture people's attention and introduce them to God's salvation (see Acts 4:30).

Why it is hard for the rich to enter the kingdom (4:4)

The king begins by admitting his self-reliance before he met God: 'I, Nebuchadnezzar, was at home in my palace, contented and prosperous' (v 4). He wants to show that he thought he did not need God. Earlier, when he had a need, he went to God, and God met the need. But because he had so much, he forgot about God and found security in his power and wealth.

The first three Gospels record Christ's statement that it is extremely hard for the rich to get into heaven (Mt 18:23–24; Mk 10:24–25; Lk 18:24–25). They also record the disciples' astonished response to that statement.

The reason why it is so hard is not that money is evil. The reason is that people with a lot of wealth think they don't need God. Sometimes they think God needs them, because they are often requested to donate to religious causes. They are self-sufficient, and it is difficult for them to exercise the childlike faith that is necessary to enter the kingdom of God. Some would even defiantly proclaim that they have no use for God; that God is needed only by weak people.

Why some people hate to seek God's help (4:5-9)

Despite Nebuchadnezzar's strong self-reliance, like before, a dream was enough to terrify him. His security came from a source that was not stable. He says, 'As I was lying in my bed, the images and visions that passed through my mind terrified me' (v 5). Again he asks help from the wise men, and again they are unable to help him (vs 6–7). 'Finally,' he says, 'Daniel came into my presence and I told him the dream' (v 8).

Then Nebuchadnezzar says something very interesting about Daniel, 'He is called Belteshazzar, after the name of my god, and the spirit of the holy gods is in him' (v 8). Here Nebuchadnezzar speaks like a polytheist. This would cast doubts on whether he was really converted. On the other hand he may be recording the way he thought at the time this happened; that is, before his conversion. That is an accepted style in story-telling even today.

Nebuchadnezzar says he knew that 'the spirit of the holy gods' was in Daniel. When he was in trouble, he knew he could go to Daniel for help. Some people may scoff at

Christians because of their principles. But when they are in trouble and don't know where to turn, they often go to committed Christians for help. They know that despite our strange beliefs, we genuinely care.

Many years ago a card-carrying member of the Communist Party came regularly to a youth club I served in. He argued a lot with us about Christianity and seemed very far from the kingdom of God. But when there was a serious sickness in his family, he contacted us, much to our surprise. He knew that in his hour of need he could trust us to be concerned for him. It was not long before he became a Christian, and later he became a dynamic leader in his church.

The fact that such people often become Christians helps us to endure the ridicule that comes our way because of our beliefs. It also motivates us to be polite and kind to those who despise us. We are tempted to break contact altogether with such people. But if we avoid that temptation, we can make the most of opportunities to minister to them when they are receptive.

Nebuchadnezzar's trust in Daniel's ability comes out clearly in the way he addresses him: 'Belteshazzar, chief of the magicians, I know that the spirit of the holy gods is in you, and no mystery is too difficult for you. Here is my dream; interpret it for me' (v 9).

Yet it is strange that Nebuchadnezzar waited so long before asking Daniel for help. He had much faith in Daniel's ability, Daniel was chief of the magicians, and this was a particularly terrifying dream. Then why was Daniel consulted last of all, even though he was easily accessible?

The text does not say the king summoned Daniel, but that Daniel came to him. Some say the king may have forgotten about the incident some years before, when Daniel interpreted a dream for him. But that is most unlikely. E. J. Young asks, 'If the king had forgotten his previous experience, would not the present dream have served, rather, to call it to mind?'[2]

John Calvin seems to have found the real reason for the king's delay when he said it was because the king was a proud man. In his address to Daniel, he appears to be very humble. But, says Calvin, he came to this point only because he was forced to do so. All other avenues to solve the problem had failed. Daniel was his last resort. E. J. Young writes, 'His dream apparently caused him to realise that he would suffer humiliation, and probably this humiliation would be at the hands of Daniel's God.'[3]

What a sad thing it is that, as Matthew Henry points out, 'many make God's word their last refuge, and never have recourse to it till they are driven off from all other succours.'[4] Paul describes the unbeliever's attitude as one of 'stubbornness' and an 'unrepentant heart' (Rom 2:5). Many would rather ruin their lives completely than turn to God for help. That is how much they want to guard their independence from God. Fortunately, Nebuchadnezzar finally swallows his pride and turns to God for help.

Confronting the arrogant with God's sovereignty (4:10–18)

Nebuchadnezzar says his dream was about an enormous and strong tree whose top touched the sky (vs 10–11). 'Its leaves were beautiful, its fruit abundant, and on it was food for all. Under it the beasts of the field found shelter, and the birds of the air lived in its branches; from it every creature was fed' (v 12). Then 'a messenger, a holy one, coming down from heaven' orders the tree cut down, so that 'the animals flee from under it and the birds from its branches' (vs 13–14). Only 'the stump and its roots, bound with iron and bronze, remain in the ground, in the grass of the field' (v 15).

After talking about the tree (vs 10–15), the messenger switches to talking about a person who is described as 'him' (vs 15–16). Daniel's interpretation of the dream explains this. The tree is King Nebuchadnezzar (v 22). So the person in verse 15 is also the king. The messenger says, 'Let him be drenched with the dew of heaven, and let him live with the animals among the plants of the earth. Let his mind be changed from that of a man and let him be given a mind of an animal, till seven times pass by for him' (vs 15–16). From Daniel's interpretation we see that what is being described is Nebuchadnezzar's temporary fall and insanity.

The purpose of his fall is given next. It is 'so that the living may know that the Most High is sovereign over the kingdoms of men and gives them to anyone he wishes and sets over them the lowliest of men' (v 17). The message given to the self-sufficient and arrogant Nebuchadnezzar is that God is 'the Most High' and 'is sovereign over the kingdoms of men.'

Arrogant people need to be confronted with this message. They need to know that God is 'Most High', that he is above everything in the universe and rules over all. Most powerful people who are unbelievers think God is for the weak. They think they don't need God, because they are 'self-made' people. They were able to come to the top without God, so why do they need him now? So the message of God's love often leaves them unimpressed. That is what I found out in my encounter with the businessman at the YFC parents' evening.

I am determined to preach God's love to all people. Not only is it the heart of the gospel, it is also the gospel's greatest attraction. A hard-hearted person may resist it. But during difficult times, the hardest heart can become vulnerable to the Spirit's wooing and suddenly see the glory of God's love.

Evangelist R. A. Torrey (1856–1928) tells how he 'was dealing with one of the most careless and vile women [he] ever met.' She moved in high society, but she had a secret life that was very immoral. Torrey says, 'She told me her story of her life in a most shameless and unblushing way, half laughing as she said it.' Torrey's response was simply to ask her to read John 3:16: 'For God so loved the world, that he gave his only begotten Son, that whosoever believeth in him shall not perish, but have everlasting life' (KJV). Dr Torrey says that 'before she had read the passage through, she burst into tears, her heart broken by the love of God to her.'[5] Something in that verse struck a responsive chord in that hard heart.

When I studied the life of Nebuchadnezzar, I began to feel it had something to say to the businessman who was unimpressed by the gospel of God's love. Because the power of God got through to this powerful king, I felt the businessman needed to be told about God's power and authority, too. Powerful people respect power. They may treat the weak with disdain. But wisdom tells them they need to negotiate wisely with the powerful. If they realise that God is the most powerful Being a person can encounter, and that someday they will face him at the judgement, then they will conclude, if they are wise, that the safest thing to do is to get on to God's side!

Nebuchadnezzar, however, did not come to that conclusion after he received this message from God. Daniel urged him to repent (v 27), but he went back to his old life. Twelve months later, the terrible things mentioned in the dream took place. Only then did he repent and acknowledge God's sovereignty.

How could Nebuchadnezzar forget such a vivid message so soon? We have seen that his basic problem was pride. As long as he was proud, he had no room for God in his life. In fact, just before his fall he says, 'Is not this the great Babylon I have built as the royal residence, by my mighty power and for the glory of my majesty' (v 30). He found satisfaction in his achievements and refused to accept that he needed help from anyone. With such an attitude, he would not seek God's favour. He had to be brought down before God could finally penetrate his hard heart. C. S. Lewis has said, 'A proud man is always looking down on things and people; and, of course, as long as you're looking down, you can't see something that's above you.'[6]

STUDY QUESTIONS

4:1   Are there any people in society or in your workplace whom you presently regard as unconvertable? Why? How can you begin praying regularly for their conversion?

4:2–3   Do you think it is appropriate to ask God to reveal himself to an unbeliever through answered prayers or signs? Why or why not?

4:4–9   What successful people do you know who think they do not need God? How might you set the stage for them to come to you for help when they face a crisis? (Often Christians have cut off links with such people so that this is not possible.)

      When have you seen people resist going to God or to his people because of stubbornness? When have you seen Christians suffer because they ignored the advice of others and refused to admit they made a mistake?

4:10–18   In what ways might you confront arrogant people with the great power of God? (This is a difficult task, but it is worth pursuing.)

9

Witnessing to the Powerful

Daniel 4:19–37

Anthony Ashley-Cooper (1801–1885), better known as the Earl of Shaftesbury, was one of the most influential politicians in nineteenth-century Britain. He was responsible for numerous laws that protected the rights of the poor, the labour force of Britain, exploited children, and the insane. When the coffin bearing his mortal remains was carried out of Westminster Abbey, a 'poor labouring man in tattered garments, but a piece of crepe sewed on his sleeve' as a sign of mourning, stood among the large crowd that had gathered. He said, 'Our Earl's gone! God a'mighty knows he loved us, and we loved him. We shan't see his likes again!'[1]

Shaftesbury's commitment to the poor and the oppressed sprang out of his commitment to Christ. But he did not grow up in a Christian home. His wealthy parents had little time for him, owing to their involvement in politics and the social life of upper-class England. But an elderly maid, Maria Mills, cared for him with the love and devotion of a mother. She introduced him to her Saviour, and that introduction helped change the course of British history. Shaftesbury carried Maria's gold watch until his death and would say, 'That was given me by the best friend I ever had.'[2]

When the great leader of the Methodist revival, John Wesley (1703–1791), was a student at Oxford University, he had a conversation with one of the servants there which 'convinced him that there was something in religion he had not grasped.' The 'janitor possessed but one coat and had not had anything to eat that day. Even though he had tasted nothing but water, he was still full of thanks to God.' Wesley told him, 'You thank God when you have nothing to wear, nothing to eat, and no bed to lie upon. What else do you thank him for?' The servant answered, 'I thank him that he has given me life and being; and a heart to love him, and a desire to serve him.'[3] That troubled Wesley, for though he was a student of divinity, he could not testify to such an experience of God. But when he did experience the Lord many years later, he set Britain ablaze with the gospel.

Some may wonder how they could possibly influence powerful people. But history attests that God often uses unknown Christians to lead famous people to Christ.

Personal concern empowers our witness
(4:19–20)

We ended the last chapter at the point where Nebuchadnezzar had completed telling Daniel about his dream. Daniel seems to have gone into deep shock when he heard about the dream. Verse 19 says, 'Then Daniel (also called Belteshazzar) was greatly perplexed for a time, and his thoughts terrified him.' The king reassures him and says, 'Belteshazzar, do not let the dream or its meaning alarm you.' Daniel's response shows that he was very concerned about Nebuchadnezzar's welfare. He says, 'My lord, if only the dream applied to your enemies and its meaning to your adversaries!' (v 19). He seems to have genuinely loved and wanted the best for his employer.

That is not the typical attitude employees have toward selfish and powerful employers. Usually they dislike them intensely, though they may mask their true feelings in order to succeed in the company. That is also not the typical attitude of people from minority communities toward those from the majority community. Usually those in the minority work hard, protect themselves, and help those in their community, but they do little for the welfare of the majority community. They are always afraid of losing the little they have, so they don't want to be concerned for the welfare of 'outsiders'.

But Christians cannot act that way. Whether we are employers or employees, whether we are from the majority community or the minority community, we should be concerned for others because we are a missionary people. Because we have received God's salvation, we should turn our attention to others, especially those in need, and look for opportunities to share the love of Christ with them. Jesus said, 'As the father has sent me, I am sending you.' Our ambition is to obey that command.

William Booth (1829–1912) was the founder of the Salvation Army, a movement that has been a model of obedience to Christ's command to care for the needs of others. It is said that when he was very old, he could not attend an anniversary meeting of the Army. So he sent a telegram that was to be opened only at the meeting. When they opened it, there was only one word in it: 'Others'. That one word sums up Christian ambition.

In Daniel's concern for Nebuchadnezzar, we see a key to effective witness: loving concern for unbelievers. There can be no adequate witness without the use of words. But our words will be much more powerful if they are backed by personal concern for the lost.

Personal confrontation completes our witness
(4:20–27)

Daniel explains the dream to Nebuchadnezzar in verses 20 to 26. Nebuchadnezzar is the great tree, and he has great power. But the tree is going to be cut down so that only a stump and the roots remain. Daniel tells Nebuchadnezzar the awful interpretation of this: 'You will be driven away from people and will live with the wild animals; you will eat grass like cattle and be drenched with the dew of heaven' (v 25).

This state will go on for a period described as 'seven times'. Alan Millard says that 'the Aramaic for "times" means a "specific period", in this case undefined.' He says that 'nothing favours years over seasons or any other measurement'.[4] Joyce Baldwin thinks the uncertainty of the duration is intentional. The king is told it will be 'until you acknowledge that the Most High is sovereign over the kingdoms of men and gives them to anyone he wishes' (v 25). The command to leave a stump is a sign that when he acknowledges that 'Heaven rules', his kingdom will be restored to him (v 26).

Daniel does not stop with the interpretation. He calls Nebuchadnezzar to repent: 'Therefore, O king, be pleased to accept my advice: Renounce your sins by doing what is right, and your wickedness by being kind to the oppressed. It may be that then your prosperity will continue' (v 27). We show concern to people. We answer their questions. We explain the gospel to them. But the work of witness is not complete until we urge them to respond to God in repentance and faith.

Sometimes we stop after we have answered questions people have asked us. And often the reason we stop at this stage is that going beyond it may be uncomfortable and awkward. It is good to start with questions people ask, but our work is not complete until we ask them *the vital question* of how they will respond to the message of Jesus.

Some people say this is unfair. They say we are exploiting a situation when people come to us with problems and we dump on them a gospel they didn't ask about. This could be called 'exploitation' if it was done for our benefit or caused harm to the other party. But what we are doing is far from that. When a doctor tells a child a story and quietly slips in an injection without the child knowing about it, we don't call that exploitation. And, in Christian witness, there is no question of secretly slipping in something. We are open about everything we do. After having won a hearing, we tell them what they need most to hear.

Someone might ask whether we would help these people in their need if we knew they would not listen to our gospel presentation. The answer is a resounding 'Yes!' We help people because we love them. When we see a need, we want to meet that need. But we also see a greater need, which is the need for a Saviour. It is natural for us, as loving people, to try to meet that greater need also.

But we will not force anyone to accept the gospel. We will not use trickery, like the doctor with the injection. The gospel cannot be communicated in that way. God respects our freedom of choice and reasons with us without ramming his message down our throats (Is 1:18). So we, too, respect people's God-given ability to choose the path they want, and we seek to persuade them about the truth without manipulating them or imposing our views on them.[5]

Like Daniel, we must urge people to turn from their wicked ways and come to the Lord of the universe. When the evangelist R. A. Torrey was in Australia, 'a man built like a prize fighter' came to him and said, 'I am not a Christian, but I am moral, upright, honourable, and blameless... and I'd like to know what you have against me.' Torrey looked at the man straight in the eye and replied, 'I charge you, sir, with high treason against Heaven's King.'[6]

We must confront people with social sin (4:27)

Daniel tells Nebuchadnezzar, 'Renounce your... wickedness by being kind to the oppressed' (v 27). This is not the type of sin we ask people to repent of in our evangelistic ministry today. Our understanding of sin is often confined to what we call personal sins. But concern for the poor is a theme that is repeated over and over again in the Scriptures.[7] The result of this neglect has been that Christians, especially Evangelicals, have often taken the side of oppressive regimes simply because they were 'right wing'. We also have seen that some supposedly committed Christians have displayed very unbiblical attitudes toward the poor in their homes, their places of work, and even in their churches.

We must challenge people to repent of both social sins and personal sins. Those who exploit their workers, who use unethical business practices, whose behaviour encourages the perpetuation of race, class, and caste distinctions, who act with injustice toward members of the opposite sex, who encourage injustice to the unborn through abortion, or who encourage the moral enslavement of individuals through pornography must be urged to repent of their sin.

Evangelicals have a wonderful heritage of battling social sin.[8] Again, William Wilberforce and the Clapham leaders provide an excellent example because of their battle against slavery in Britain in the eighteenth and nineteenth centuries. This is how Richard Lovelace describes it:

> The Clapham leaders habitually spent three hours in prayer daily, and Christians all over England united in prayer on the eve of the critical debates. Other means used included cease-less publicising of the evils of slavery, the gatherings of peti-tions from all over the country, and even the boycott of slave produced goods.... Wilberforce's inspired oratory helped reach and compel the conscience of Parliament.[9]

Recently we have seen Christians in the United States see encouraging results in their battle against pornography. Charles Colson tells the exciting story of how Jack Eckerd, the founder of the large Eckerd drugstore chain, helped in this. He walked through one of his drugstores shortly after he became a Christian in 1983 'and saw with new eyes the pornographic magazines on sale there.' He called the com-pany president and told him, 'Take the magazines out.' He was stunned because these magazines brought in several million dollars of profit a year. But Eckerd prevailed, and the magazines were taken off the racks of the 1,700 Eckerd drugstores. This started a process that accelerated the removal of pornographic magazines from many other chains of stores.

Colson says he 'called Jack and asked if he had pitched the pornography because of his conversion to Christ.' 'Of course,' he replied, 'Why else would I throw a few million dollars out of the window? But as I thought about it, the Lord wouldn't let me off the hook.' Colson says, 'He was simply yielding to the Lordship of Christ.'[10]

A crisis must be followed by a process (4:28–30)

God gave Nebuchadnezzar twelve months to repent. But he refused to do so. 'Twelve months later, as the king was walking on the roof of the royal palace of Babylon, he said, "Is not this the great Babylon I have built as the royal residence, by my mighty power and for the glory of my majesty?"' (v 30). Still he is as stubbornly proud as ever.

How people can neglect the call of God! The call to repent came very clearly to Nebuchadnezzar. Considering how terrified he had been and how powerful he knew God was, I'm sure Nebuchadnezzar took God's warning seriously at the time. He may even have accepted Daniel's advice with gratitude! But he did not do anything about it. For him, it was the time for action, the time to change his way. Instead, Nebuchadnezzar went back to his ordinary life. There was no clear-cut break with the past after his crisis experience, and soon the experience itself was forgotten.

How often God speaks to people and, in the heat of the moment, they resolve to change their way of life. But as they go back to their daily routine, one compromise after another is made until, finally, all the crisis leaves behind is an awkward memory. Someone has said that a crisis that is not followed by a process becomes an abscess.

Some are converted only after a long time (4:31–37)

After twelve months, all that was prophesied through the dream takes place. Nebuchadnezzar becomes like an animal, and he lives in the wild until the 'seven times' pass (vs 31–33). He writes about what happened after that in this way: 'At the end of that time, I, Nebuchadnezzar, raised my eyes toward heaven, and my sanity was restored. Then I praised the Most High; I honoured and glorified him who lives forever' (v 34).

Next follows a poem of praise (vs 34–35). Then he says how he was given back the glory he had before: 'I was restored to my throne and became even greater than before' (v 36). The last verse of the chapter is another expression of praise to God from Nebuchadnezzar (v 37).

It took a long time before Nebuchadnezzar was converted. He was subjected to many experiences over an extended period of time before he finally yielded to God's claims. But this is often the way with evangelism among the unreached. People without much of a background of Christianity often take some time before they respond. There is so much wrong thinking that has to be cleared and so much stubbornness that the Spirit of God has to hammer away at.

Leighton Ford tells about a young pastor friend of his who led a hardened criminal to Christ in a county jail. This man told him, 'Now, preacher, don't get the big head because I have accepted Christ. You are just the twenty-fifth man.' The preacher asked him what he meant by that. 'Well,' he said, 'I can think of at least twenty-four others who have witnessed to me about Christ. And it was the effect of this that finally led me to Christ. You just happened to be the twenty-fifth.'[11] So sometimes we are just one link in the chain that leads to a person's conversion.

Sometimes God calls us to minister to the same people over an extended period of time before they are converted. One day a preacher visited a leprosy hospital and, while talking to the people there, met one person who had a vital, glowing love for Jesus. They struck up a conversation, and the patient told the preacher, 'You know I didn't always have this joy and love for God in my heart. When I first came to this hospital, I was the most angry and bitter man here. But one man from the village nearby came out every day to visit me and bring me food.' (In our part of the world, hospital food is usually of poor quality.)

The man said that, at first, he threw the food back in the visitor's face. 'He'd come out and offer to play cards with me, but I shouted at him to leave me alone. He wanted to talk to me, but I would say nothing to him. Still he kept coming to visit me, day after day after day.' Finally the man asked this person, '*Why* do you keep coming to see me, when all I ever show you is bitterness and hatred?' The man replied that it was because of the love of Christ.

The preacher asked the leper, 'How long did your friend from the village come to see you before you gave your heart to Christ?' He answered, 'He came every day for thirteen years.'[12] He persevered, and in the end he saw fruit. So, in the work of evangelism, the advice of Paul in Galatians 6:9 is very appropriate: 'Let us not become weary in doing good, for at the proper time we will reap a harvest if we do not give up.'

STUDY QUESTIONS

4:19–20   Why is it difficult to show concern to people who are wealthy,powerful, and arrogant? Think of a few such people. In what specific ways can you show them Christian concern?

Committed Christians are almost always a minority community. How can we ensure that we don't fall into the trap of unconcern for outsiders?

4:20–27   When witnessing to unbelievers, have you ever felt reluctant to move from discussing issues to the step of confrontation? If you have, what reasons can you give for this reluctance?

4:27   What social sins must we challenge people — especially the rich — to repent of today?

Have you unconsciously taken on a social sin that you need to repent of?

4:28–30   How can the impact of a spiritual crisis be diminished by failing to follow through with what you learned in that crisis? (Give examples.)

4:31–37   How does the length of time before Nebuchadnezzar came to God encourage you about your witness to resistant people? Take time to pray about the salvation of these resistant people.

10

People Who Don't Care about God

Daniel 5:1–31

A student in Sri Lanka acted in what seemed like a very carefree manner. He was a favourite among the girls and had a great sense of humour. He was a good sportsman and was relatively good in his studies. A Christian friend tried to share the gospel with him. But he brushed off this witness carelessly as something irrelevant to him. One day the Christian told him that if he did not repent he would go to hell. His friend laughed and said that was where he wanted to go. He would be a stranger in heaven, he said. Besides, all his friends would be in hell. They could get together and have a fine time there!

I'm sure you have met such people. They exude so much confidence and satisfaction that you wonder whether they would listen to your ideas about their need for a Saviour. Daniel 5 presents a king called Belshazzar who seemed to have the carefree attitude of the person just described.

Who was King Belshazzar?

Before we look at the story of King Belshazzar, it would be good to discuss some questions that have arisen about his identity. There is no record outside the Bible of a king of Babylon by this name, and the last king of Babylon is known to have been Nabonidus. This fact has been used to discount the historical accuracy of Daniel and as evidence for the theory that this book was written some centuries after the sixth century BC, which was when the events in Daniel are supposed to have taken place.

In some cuneiform texts, discovered by archaeologists in the middle of the nineteenth century, Belshazzar is mentioned as being the son of Nabonidus.[1] Nabonidus was at war in Arabia for about ten years of his seventeen-year reign, and he did not return until after the fall of Babylon. Alan Millard describes the findings as follows: '[Belshazzar] exercised royal authority during his father's absence and is named beside him in the oath formulae' of that reign. 'The word "king", moreover, enjoyed a wider use than in English.'[2] Joyce Baldwin points to the fact that the reward given to Daniel for reading the mysterious writing on the wall was to be made third highest ruler in the kingdom (5:16,29). That would make sense if 'King' Belshazzar was the second highest ruler.

Objections have been made also because Belshazzar is described as Nebuchadnezzar's son. Again, as Millard points out, 'a looser use of "father" may be involved than English can allow.' It is quite possible that Belshazzar's mother was Nebuchadnezzar's daughter. It was she who reminded Belshazzar about Nebuchadnezzar's trusted confidant, Daniel. If this was so, Nebuchadnezzar was a grandfather to Belshazzar. Besides, as Gleason Archer points out, 'The ancient Semitic languages termed any predecessor in office as the "father" of his immediate or mediate successor.'[3]

We add a word of caution that there is little historical evidence about this period outside what is found in the Bible. Millard says, 'The Babylonian kings have left very incomplete accounts of their reigns.' That should make us cautious about claiming complete authority for the explanations of the problems relating to King Belshazzar. It is also wise to be cautious about using issues like this to dismiss stories in the Bible as being historically inaccurate. Often the confident claims of those who discount the historical reliability of the Bible have been thrown out by archaeological and other discoveries like the one that indicated Belshazzar was the son of Nabonidus.

The deceptive pleasures of rebellion (5:1–12)

'King Belshazzar gave a great banquet for a thousand of his nobles' (v 1). He took the goblets King Nebuchadnezzar brought from the temple in Jerusalem and gave them to his guests for wine glasses (vs 2–3).

He demonstrates a careless disregard for the things of God. He was the powerful king of the land. He knew about God's dealings with Nebuchadnezzar (see verse 22). But he had no respect for God or his people, so he did something abominable to them.

The Jews who knew what was happening must have felt humiliated, just as Christians who are in a minority feel when others enjoy sinful indulgence, and they are ridiculed because they will not participate.

Verse 4 says, 'As they drank the wine, they praised the gods of gold and silver, or bronze, iron, wood and stone.' Here is a direct affront to God's sovereignty. People are drinking out of vessels from God's temple and praising man-made idols. It is one of the many times in this book where people despise the things of God with a triumphant show of arrogance.

We don't know the reason for the banquet, but at that very time the armies of the Persian ruler Cyrus were closing in on Babylon and were encamped outside the city walls. Was Belshazzar so confident that he ignored the threat? Gleason Archer writes, 'Babylon was considered impregnable because of its magnificent fortifications.... The city had not been stormed by invaders in over a thousand years.'[4] Joyce Baldwin thinks the 'banquet was sheer bravado, the last fling of a terrified ruler unsuccessfully attempting to drown his fears.'[5]

Whatever the motive behind the revelry may have been, the king's arrogance was shattered when 'suddenly the fingers of a human hand appeared and wrote on the plaster of the wall, near the lampstand in the royal palace.

The king watched the hand as it wrote. His face turned pale and he was so frightened that his knees knocked together and his legs gave way' (vs 5–6). This fearful reaction is typical of a person who tries to fight with God. Belshazzar knew about the one true God and about Nebuchadnezzar's encounters with him (vs 18–22). Yet he thought he could rebel against God. He seemed to be in control and was in a state of revelry when suddenly he realised that he had built his life on something very insecure.

Sometimes when Christians see unbelievers revelling in their life of sin and rebellion, they are tempted to envy them. In some circles, people ridicule those who remain faithful to principles of holiness. Young people sometimes use the word *virgin* to insult another, because a virgin is thought to have missed out on one of life's essential pleasures. Yet that front of confidence is very thin. A small thing is often enough to bring misery to such people. They should be pitied, not envied.

In typical fashion, King Belshazzar calls his enchanters, astrologers, and diviners and promises great rewards — including the third highest position in the kingdom — to the one who can read the writing on the wall and explain what it means (v 7). 'But they could not read the writing or tell the king what it meant. So King Belshazzar became even more terrified and his face grew more pale. His nobles were baffled' (vs 8–9).

Then the queen, who is probably the king's mother, comes in and tells him about Daniel: 'Don't be alarmed! Don't look so pale! There is a man in your kingdom who has the spirit of the holy gods in him' (vs 10–11). She tells him about Daniel's service for Nebuchadnezzar and about his abilities (vs 11–12). Then she says, 'Call for Daniel, and he will tell you what the writing means' (v 12).

Daniel must have been deeply distressed at the time of the banquet because of the dishonour brought to his God. It was also a time of personal defeat for him, for the reforms he had worked so hard to bring about were being rejected. You can imagine his surprise when a delegation came from the king, treated him with great respect, and asked him to come and help the king out of his crisis.

The queen had said, 'There is a man in your kingdom who has the spirit of the holy gods in him.' This is the same thing Nebuchadnezzar said about Daniel when he testified about his second dream (4:8). Again we see that while the world may scoff at us and ridicule our principles, they cannot help noticing that we seem to have contact with God. In their time of need, when they have nowhere to go, the very people who treat us with disdain may come to us for help.

The danger of being careless about the sacred
(5:13–23)

When Daniel is brought before Belshazzar, the king tells him that he has heard of his abilities. The king promises Daniel great rewards if he can read the writing on the wall and tell him what it means (vs 13–16). Daniel consents to do so but tells the king to keep his rewards (v 17).

After telling Belshazzar about the lesson King Nebuchadnezzar learned through his temporary insanity (vs 18–21), Daniel declares, 'But you his son, O Belshazzar, have not humbled yourself, though you knew all this' (v 22). Later he makes the same charge in a different way, 'You did not honour the God who holds in his hand your life and all your ways' (v 23).

Daniel asserts that Belshazzar is guilty of arrogant disrespect of God in two ways. 'You had the goblets from his temple brought to you, and you and your nobles, your wives and your concubines drank wine from them' (v 23). And 'you praised the gods of silver and gold, of bronze, iron, wood and stone, which cannot see or hear or understand' (v 23).

Daniel's emphasis on the second sin — idolatry — is understandable. That sin is abhorrent to God all through the Scriptures. But why was the sin of using the goblets so serious? Ronald Wallace asks, 'Why should God make such a fuss about the use of a set of golden cups from a temple he seems to have deserted — belonging to an era now well in the past?' He points out that 'it could be argued that no human being was directly harmed by what was done. No cruelty was involved — no inhumanity of man to man.'[6]

Wallace's answer to this question is enlightening. He goes on to say that in the life of Israel, God decreed certain things as being holy. The temple was such a place and, because of this, the vessels of the temple were also regarded as holy. Therefore profaning these things was considered very serious.

One might object to this reasoning and charge that we are guilty of unbiblical superstition when we speak of the importance of sacred objects. But there are many places in the Old Testament where the seriousness of profaning symbols of God's holiness is presented. It surprises us to find the sons of Aaron, Nadab and Abihu, killed on the spot for offering 'unauthorised fire before the LORD' (Lev 10:1–2). At their consecration ceremony they had failed to keep the regulations given by God, and they were immediately put to death. Strong punishments are mentioned repeatedly for those who profane the Sabbath.

The New Testament also contains important symbols. For example, the symbol of the Lord's Supper reminds us of God's grace revealed on the cross. The symbol of baptism confirms that we have died to our old self and are born into God's family as new creatures. Because these and other symbols reveal the Lord's holiness, profaning them is very serious.

Paul echoes this attitude in 1 Corinthians 11 when he says, 'Whoever eats the bread or drinks the cup in an unworthy manner will be guilty of sinning against the body and blood of the Lord. A man ought to examine himself before he eats of the bread and drinks of the cup' (vs 27–28).

Of course, we should always examine ourselves. But it is particularly serious to participate in the Lord's Supper without proper spiritual preparation. Paul goes on to say that one who participates in this way 'eats and drinks judgement on himself. That is why many among you are weak and sick, and a number of you have fallen asleep' (vs 29–30).

We should regard all aids to holiness given to us by God with utmost seriousness. The church has called these 'means of grace', that is, 'media through which grace may be received[7] into our lives. Those who are careless with the symbolic means of grace God has given will invariably grow spiritually weak.

Some Christians give themselves exclusively to intellectual enrichment (belief) and service to mankind (obedience). But they neglect spiritual disciplines like observing the Lord's Day, the Lord's Supper, and seasons of prayer. Eventually they will find themselves spiritually impoverished and lacking in the joy that comes from communion with God. When we neglect the means God had ordained for our spiritual enrichment, we pay dearly for it.

When Daniel told Belshazzar he had rebelled against the Lord of heaven, the first example he gave was profaning the vessels from the Lord's temple. Could our carelessness with the holy institutions ordained by God also express disrespect to God, if not outright rebellion?

The consequence of carelessness is judgement
(5:24–30)

In verses 24 to 28 Daniel explains the meaning of what was written on the wall. The words written were 'MENE, MENE, TEKEL, PARSIN' (v 25). Daniel read the signs as Aramaic words for units of weight or currency: 'A mina, a mina, a shekel and fractions'.

What Daniel did with these words was to interpret them by punning, which was 'a favourite device among Babylonian scholars'.[8] If the wise men of the king's court could have read these words, they would have understood them as nouns indicating weights or currency. But Daniel, under the inspiration of God and using the technique of punning, read their verbal forms: 'Numbered, numbered, weighed, divided'.

The procedure seems strange to us, partly because we can't hear the words pronounced and so sense the punning. But to the people of that time, it would have been plausible. This type of thing happens today when people make double-meaning jokes. Some catch the meaning and laugh, while others wonder what was so funny. Similarly

Daniel caught the meaning of this statement through punning, while the other wise men did not.

Daniel's procedure of interpretation yielded the following meaning:

- *Mene:* God has numbered the days of your reign and brought it to an end.
- *Tekel:* You have been weighed on the scales and found wanting.
- *Peress:* Your kingdom is divided and given to the Medes and Persians (vs 26–28).

This was a clear message of judgement to the king. Interestingly, Daniel is rewarded for what he has done (v 29). But he has little time to enjoy the rewards, because his prophecy is fulfilled immediately. 'That very night Belshazzar, king of the Babylonians, was slain, and Darius the Mede took over the kingdom, at the age of sixty-two' (vs 30–31).

We started this chapter by describing the confidence of people who don't care about God, which is how Daniel 5 begins. We end the chapter the way Daniel 5 ends, by describing the destiny of such people — judgement. Daniel is not afraid to tell this king that he is doomed and that judgement will come on him soon.

Do we think of people who don't care about God as headed for a fearful judgement? Any reading of Scripture would yield such a conviction. If we believed this and had any sense of responsibility or love for these people, we would warn them that 'it is a dreadful thing to fall into the hands of the living God' (Heb 10:31). Some may laugh and make a joke of the warning, as did the student mentioned at the start of this chapter. Others may even reward us, as Belshazzar did to Daniel.[9] Whatever their response, people headed for a terrible judgement are not to be envied but pitied.

STUDY QUESTIONS

5:1–12   Have you ever been tempted to envy powerful and arrogant unbelievers? Why? How did you (or should you) overcome this envy?

Belshazzar's reign was a time of great personal defeat for Daniel because the reforms he had brought about were rejected. Have you or other Christians you know had to face similar earthly failure? What keeps a Christian going at such times?

5:13–23   Why have evangelical Christians generally ignored symbols that reveal God's holiness? How might Christian symbols help you in your walk with God?

5:24–30   When you encounter difficult statements in the Bible like *Mene, Mene, Tekel, Parsin* (5:25), what do you do? What procedures should you adopt to try and understand what they mean?

What harmful effects in the church and in society might result from neglecting the doctrine of judgement?

CHAPTER

11

When Good People Come under Fire

Daniel 6:1–10

During the early days of the Salvation Army, William Booth and his associates were often attacked in the press by religious leaders and government leaders alike. When his son, Bramwell, showed Booth a newspaper attack, he would reply, 'Bramwell, fifty years hence it will matter very little indeed how these people treated us; it will matter a great deal how we dealt with the work of God.'[1]

We often associate Christlikeness with being likeable. But when we look at the life of Jesus, we see that many people disliked and even hated him. Daniel, too, had enemies who plotted his death. That should not surprise us, for Paul said, 'Everyone who wants to live a godly life in Christ Jesus will be persecuted' (2 Tim 3:12). In this chapter the top officials of King Darius seek to entrap Daniel.

Who was Darius the Mede?

Daniel 6 begins with Daniel in a position of leadership in the regime of the Medo-Persian king, Darius the Mede. He is said to have taken over the kingdom from Belshazzar at the age of sixty-two (5:31). Historians are quite certain that the one who did take over at this time was Cyrus the Great, when he was about sixty years of age.

There was a time when certain critical scholars confidently asserted that the reference to Darius here was evidence of the historical inaccuracy of the book. There was a king called Darius Hystaspes who reigned much later. It was assumed that the writer of Daniel was so confused about the history of the sixth century BC that he thought this Darius Hystaspes preceded Cyrus.

Other scholars have risen in defence of Daniel's historical accuracy with very plausible explanations. It has been pointed out, for example, that by calling this person Darius the Mede, and by saying that he took over at age sixty-two, the writer was clearly distinguishing him from Darius Hystaspes who began to reign in his twenties. J. C. Whitcomb points out that 'the book of Daniel gives far more information concerning the personal background of Darius the Mede than of Belshazzar or even Nebuchadnezzar. For he is the only monarch whose age, parentage and nationality are recorded.'[2] It would be very unwise to reject the historicity of Darius, of whom so much is said, especially after the writer of Daniel was vindicated regarding the identity of Belshazzar, as we saw in chapter 10.

Who, then, was Darius the Mede? The esteemed British Assyriologist D. J. Wiseman suggests that he was Cyrus the Great, whom other sources state as having conquered Babylon. The ages of Cyrus and Darius at the time of conquest tally (early sixties). Wiseman gives various reasons why we could take Darius as another name for Cyrus.[3] J. C. Whitcomb suggests that Darius is another name for Gubaru, who was the governor of Babylon and other regions and who could be properly called a king because he exercised powers very much like those of a king.[4]

So we cannot say for sure who Darius was. But we will not declare, as some do, that the use of this name is evidence that the book of Daniel is historically inaccurate.[5]

Facing opposition when we expect praise (6:1-4)

King Darius is said to have appointed '120 satraps [or "kingdom protectors"] to rule throughout the kingdom, with three administrators over them, one of whom was Daniel' (vs 1–2). 'Now Daniel so distinguished himself among the administrators and the satraps by his exceptional qualities that the king planned to set him over the whole kingdom. At this, the administrators and the satraps tried to find grounds for charges against Daniel in his conduct of government affairs, but they were unable to do so' (vs 3–4).

It was a case of professional jealousy! From all we know of him, Daniel seems to have been a polite and respectful person. But he was also a capable person. He got things done, and was recognised for his achievements. So he climbed the social ladder very fast. Such people become vulnerable to criticism. If you don't want to be criticised, stay away from doing anything significant. Just be a nice person who 'sticks to the book' and does not try to cut any new ground in your field of service. But if you do something significant, you can be sure you will be criticised for it.

Sometimes opposition comes to us from good people who can't understand what we are trying to do. The Salvation Army has had an exciting history of service and evangelism among the poor and needy. Yet the Earl of Shaftesbury, who was also a great defender of the poor, once 'announced that, after much study, he was convinced that the Salvation Army was clearly antichrist. Then some admirer of the Earl announced that in his own studies he learned that the "number" of William Booth's name added up to 666!'[6]

That type of criticism will hurt you, especially if you have gone out of your way to be polite and kind to everyone you meet. It breaks your heart to find that you are the object of criticism for the very thing you thought would bring you praise.

But don't be disillusioned. We don't work for praise on earth. Our desire is to do the will of God. That will includes being loving and respectful of all people. If we have fulfilled those conditions, then we can be satisfied and can try not to let criticism devastate us. In fact, as we apply the principle of God's sovereignty to the criticism, we can be assured that God will use it for our ultimate good.

Being blameless before the world (6:3–4)

Darius may have heard that Daniel had 'the spirit of the holy gods in him' (5:11). Although he had been a trusted advisor in the defeated kingdom, his long experience in government would have made him a good man to have around. But Daniel must have been over eighty years old at this time.[7] So it comes as a surprise to read that Darius made him something like the prime minister of the kingdom. Verse 3 gives his 'exceptional qualities' as the reason for Daniel's promotion. What Darius saw was a person of great ability and experience.

Daniel was also a person of good character. One of the tragedies in today's political arenas is that people of great abilities are not always people of good character. Many people assume that you cannot climb the social ladder if you are a 'good person'; that is, one who is completely honest, principled, kind, and unselfish. Daniel disproves that assumption.

'The administrators and the satraps tried to find grounds for charges against Daniel in his conduct of government affairs, but they were unable to do so' (v 4). I wish that what is said about him next could be said of all Christians: 'They could find no corruption in him, because he was trustworthy and neither corrupt nor negligent' (v 4). He was blameless before his critics.

At least thirteen times in the New Testament Christians are told to live blamelessly before the world.[8] Our character becomes particularly important if we are going to take unpopular stands and come under fire. And if we take seriously Christ's call to be salt and light in the world (Mt 5:13–16), we will be disliked because of the stands we take.

The young church leader Timothy came under fire from the church. His opponents used his youth to try and disqualify him from leadership. Paul's advice to him was, 'Don't let anyone look down on you because you are young, but set an example for the believers in speech, in life, in love, in faith and in purity' (1 Tim 4:12).

George Mueller was active in itinerant ministry until he was about eighty-eight years old. One of the reasons he gave for his preservation was 'the exercising of himself to have always a conscience void of offence both toward God and toward men' (Acts 24:16).[9]

We lose our spiritual freedom when we live with unsettled matters and secret sins. They become such a drain on us that we soon lose the freshness of the Holy Spirit's infilling. Such people do not have the spiritual and mental energy to persevere in serving God at old age.

I must add that there is always hope for people to be used by God after they have made big mistakes or committed shameful acts. But such people must accept responsibility for their sins and not be afraid to confess them in public, if necessary. Then they are free to be filled with God's Spirit and used by him. We see this in the effective ministry of Charles Colson, who was involved in the Watergate scandal in America.[10]

Three specific qualities of Daniel are mentioned in verse 4. First, he was 'trustworthy' or 'faithful' (NRSV). This quality is also given as a supreme requirement for Christian service. First Corinthians 4:2 says, 'Now it is required that those who have been given a trust must prove faithful.'

When you ask trustworthy people to do something, you can be sure that it will be done. Such people refuse to give up. When they face obstacles, they seek to overcome them.

When you give a job to untrustworthy people, they come back with excuses. They say they were unable to do it because they were too busy, or because their car broke down, or because they lacked the resources to do the job well. Of course there may be times when a job is not completed because of unavoidable circumstances. But some people simply give up too easily. They are untrustworthy.

We sometimes excuse people's ineffectiveness by saying, 'At least they are faithful.' By that we usually mean, 'They have not been dishonest.' But faithfulness means more than honesty. It also includes perseverance and the willingness to work hard, even at one's own inconvenience.

Second, Daniel is described as not 'corrupt'. First Peter 3:16 exhorts us to keep 'a clear conscience, so that those who speak maliciously against your good behaviour in Christ may be ashamed of their slander.' John Calvin says, 'Integrity is the best of all protectors.... We cannot be more secure than when fortified by a good conscience.'[11]

This world is being progressively destroyed by corruption. What force there would be if thousands of Christians were known to be so honest that they would rather face failure, poverty, and humiliation than give in to corruption. Yet recently people who have accused Christians of dishonesty have not been put to shame, as Peter said. They have been vindicated because what they said was true.

Third, we are told that Daniel was not 'negligent'.[12] The word used here means 'neglect' or 'remissness'.[13] Many good people foolishly get themselves into vulnerable situations because they have been careless. In fact, carelessness is often the root of serious sin in a Christian's life.

A Christian establishes a business partnership with a non-Christian without carefully discussing the principles they will follow. In a crisis, he finds himself being forced to do something he knows to be wrong.

A travelling salesman is careless about his choice of a hotel and has made no plans about what he will do during his free time. Later in the evening he succumbs to sexual temptation.

A person starts building a house without properly assessing how much it will cost. When he finds he is running short of money, he proceeds with his old plans without adjusting them according to his resources. He gets himself so deeply into debt that he lives in bondage and fear.

A busy woman is not careful about keeping her daily time of prayer and Bible study. She gradually makes a habit of skipping it and ends up spiritually dry and defeated.

A father spends less and less time at home because of demands in his workplace. Gradually his wife becomes discontent and his children become rebellious and disrespectful.

These are examples of how carelessness leads people into sin. That is why we should not excuse carelessness by saying it is a weakness we must live with. We should give special attention to areas of carelessness and seek to overcome them. Paul's advice about this is, 'Be very careful, then, how you live — not as unwise but as wise, making the most of every opportunity, because the days are evil' (Eph 5:15–16).

We do the will of God, even if it angers others (6:5–10)

The administrators and satraps tried hard to find fault with Daniel but found him blameless. Then they realised that there was only one area in which they could trap him: it had to be 'something to do with the law of his God' (v 5).

The particular thing they chose was prayer. They 'went as a group to the king and said: "O King Darius, live forever! The royal administrators, prefects, satraps, advisers and governors have all agreed that the king should issue an edict and enforce the decree that anyone who prays to any god or man during the next thirty days, except to you, O king, shall be thrown into the lions den"' (vs 6–7).

It was a carefully planned plot. It came from all the leaders, and all were there to present it — except, of course, Daniel. It flattered the king, and often a flattered person can be made to do things he usually objects to. This particular proposal seemed good for the stability of the empire. When the leaders pledge allegiance to the new king through prayer, it would establish him as firmly in control and, possibly, as semi-divine. Joyce Baldwin writes: 'Even if it did encroach on private, personal religious devotion, the period of the edict was limited and no possible harm could be envisaged.'[14]

What Daniel had to decide was whether he would abstain from his practice just for a month. Perhaps he could pray silently in a seated posture without getting down on his knees and facing Jerusalem near his window. Then no one would find out that he was praying. And he would save his life and save the king so much heartache and embarrassment. Yet, for Daniel, that would mean putting God in a place below the king. That he could not do. He follows his usual practice of opening his windows and praying in the sight of all who would watch (v 10) and, by so doing, condemns himself to the den of lions.

This is one of the many heroic acts which showed that to Daniel the will of God took precedence over everything else. Usually Daniel would have obeyed his leaders. That is why they loved him even though he was so faithful to his religion and his principles. As Christians, we too should usually follow Paul's advice: 'Everyone must submit himself to the governing authorities' (Rom 13:1). But when it comes to compromising the supreme place God has in our lives, we must be willing, like Daniel, to risk our lives and disobey our leaders.

We have many converts from Buddhism in our church. Sometimes they do not come for worship on Sunday because a Buddhist friend or relative has come to visit them, and they do not want to offend the relative by saying they have to go to church. In our culture, where hospitality is very important, there is a possibility that these people would be offended. But that is a price they should pay to express the place of honour they give to God. By refusing to go to church, they give the impression that God is not terribly important to them. Their relatives may not be offended, but their behaviour does nothing to help the relatives respect God either. By trying to protect a friendship, they may have lost a chance to witness about God to their friends.

Today we often see worldly people treating God with scant respect, using curse words and making bad humour that includes God. I sometimes wonder whether such people have lost their fear of God after seeing those who are supposed to be his children treating him with little respect. If they see us standing up for him at great cost to ourselves, as Daniel did, they may perhaps develop a respect for him that could lead to their salvation. It is interesting that the decree Darius issued after this episode said, 'In every part of my kingdom people must fear and reverence the God of Daniel' (v 26).

I have been greatly challenged by something I read about Sir Thomas More, who was Lord Chancellor of England in the sixteenth century. The king sent for him while he was at his prayers in public. He sent back a message that he would attend to the king after he had first performed his service to the King of kings! He was a person who had a clear understanding of his priorities in life.

Let me close this chapter with a word to anyone who has been hurt by criticism or opposition. You are not alone. All righteous people have experienced this, including Jesus himself. He understands what you are going through. So go to him and renew your strength by waiting on him (Isaiah 40:31). That is what Daniel did, as we will see in the next chapter.

STUDY QUESTIONS

6:1–4   Why do many people fall into the trap of associating Christlikeness with likeableness?

Have you had the experience of being criticised after you have worked hard on a project? What do you think were the causes for the criticism? What helped you or will help you to overcome the ill-effects of this criticism?

6:3–4   Why is it that many people who profess to be born again do not have a testimony like Daniel's at their workplace? How might the church have unwittingly contributed to this sad state of affairs by not giving instruction about discipleship in the workplace?

Can you think of a situation in your life or that of another where carelessness led to serious sin? How could that sin have been prevented?

6:5–10   In what situations might flattery lead a person to do something that later proves to be foolish?

What are some common situations in which Christians might compromise the supreme place of God in their lives rather than facing embarrassment or unpopularity or inconvenience?

Facing Trouble
through Prayer

Daniel 6:10–28

> A daily relationship with God in prayer helps us not to con-
> fuse our will with his will. Any person in public life who
> thinks he can 'go it alone' is tragically mistaken. No one has
> enough love, enough concern, enough humility, enough
> strength, enough courage. In an individual's friendship with
> God there comes each day the humility of having fallen short,
> the joy of being forgiven, and the strength of being renewed.[1]

Those words were not written by a preacher
but by a politician, Senator Mark Hatfield, around the mid-
point of his long and distinguished career in American politics. They seem to suggest that praying is the most
important ingredient for an effective Christian life.

Preachers also have been asserting the importance of
prayer for a long time. The British preacher Charles
Spurgeon (1834–1892) said, 'I could as soon think of living
without eating, or living without breathing, as living without prayer.'[2] The saintly Scottish preacher Robert Murray
McCheyne (1813–1843) said, 'What a man is on his knees
before God, that he is — and nothing more.' But it is very
significant when such a powerful affirmation of prayer

comes from Mark Hatfield who, like Daniel, has a career in public life which has spanned many decades and, despite the many unpopular stands he has taken, is always a testimony of faithfulness to Christ.

We already discussed Daniel's community prayer life in chapter 4 of this book, and we will look at one of his famous prayers in the next chapter. Now we will see what we can learn from his habit of daily prayer.

Hoping for restoration amid great gloom (6:10)

Daniel 6:10 says, 'Now when Daniel learned that the decree [outlawing prayers to anyone but King Darius] had been published, he went home to his upstairs room where the windows opened toward Jerusalem.'

Why should Daniel face Jerusalem anymore? The city was in ruins, and the temple that signified God's presence was destroyed. Yet this is where he usually prayed, expressing his belief that Jerusalem was still the city of God. Implied in this would be the hope that one day Jerusalem would be restored to its pristine glory. The book of Daniel pulsates throughout with a hope built on the belief in God's sovereignty over history. Daniel's habit of prayer facing Jerusalem is an expression of that hope.

As I first wrote these words, we were facing huge challenges in our work, and I was almost afraid to assess their magnitude. I went to the office, and my spirit recoiled at the prospect of leaving the security of the computer to go into the 'real world' of conflict and struggle.

I had originally intended to bypass in my exposition the statement about Daniel's looking toward Jerusalem. But the implication gleaned encouraged me to hope for restoration in our work, just as Daniel hoped for Jerusalem's restoration. Because our God is committed to his name and to those who bear that name, he restores us if we are obedient to him. Bless his name!

Prayer as a regular habit (6:10)

While describing how Daniel prayed, verse 10 tells us a lot about Daniel's prayer life. It says, 'Three times a day he got down on his knees and prayed, giving thanks to his God, just as he had done before.'

Often in the Scriptures we find people praying on their knees.[3] It is not the only recommended position, for sometimes people prayed standing.[4] Once Jesus fell on his face as he prayed.[5] Jesus was often seen to slip into prayer in the middle of conversation with others.[6] This evidence suggests that we should not make a rule about the ideal posture for prayer. Yet the kneeling position is neither too comfortable (to make us lethargic) nor too uncomfortable. And it helps us develop an attitude of humble reverence before God.

I think the significance of kneeling in this story is seen in the words 'just as he had done before.' This was Daniel's habit, and kneeling helped him to make this time exclusively his prayer time. As he went about his daily life, he may have prayed what have been called 'flash prayers' or prayers 'on the run', as Jesus did. But he was in the habit of separating times each day exclusively for prayer. In the same way each Christian needs to have a time that is exclusively given to communion with God. What is important is not whether we kneel or sit or walk while praying, but whether we give time exclusively for prayer.

Our prayer time is when we receive spiritual strength to live and witness in a world that does not respect spiritual reality. People who are active in such a world need this desperately so that they can go against the tide and maintain their Christian stand. Jesus told his disciples as they prepared to face a hostile mob, 'Pray that you will not fall into temptation' (Lk 22:40). Besides this, of course, is the fact that God answers prayer.

So praying for our needs and those of others is one of the most important things we can do. Yet what the American preacher Vance Hanver said some years ago is true today also: 'Many a man who would never think of dashing out in the morning without his breakfast, his vitamins and his briefcase, plunges headlong into a perilous day with an unprepared soul. "A little talk with Jesus" read-ies the body, the mind and the spirit for whatever comes.'[7]

The devotional history of many Christians could be summarised by the following sequence. In the first few years after they commit their lives to Christ, there is a rigid, almost superstitious keeping of a disciplined 'quiet time'. Then they realise that because they live under grace their rigid attitude does not harmonise with the freedom of spirit characteristic of biblical Christianity. And that is true.

The next stage in the process is when they start missing their quiet time when they are very busy. Soon they find that they have their time with God less and less frequently, until such times become rare. Next they will find that even when they have free time it is hard to slow themselves down to concentrate on prayer. They simply don't feel like praying, because they have lost the taste for prayer.

Many years ago, E. Stanley Jones said, 'If I were to put my finger on the greatest lack in American Christianity, I would unhesitatingly point to the need for an effective prayer life among laity and clergy.'[8] I believe that today this is true of Christianity worldwide.

What advice can we give to those who have lost the taste for prayer and find it difficult because they do not feel like praying? James 4:8 says, 'Come near to God and he will come near to you.' That is a promise! You must begin to pray, and once you have taken that step, God will come to you and minister to your needs. It won't be long before you snap back into a vibrant prayer life.

Charles Spurgeon has a memorable quote about this: 'I believe that when we cannot pray, it is time we prayed more than ever. And if you answer, "But, how can that be?" I would say, pray to pray. Pray for prayer. Pray for the spirit of supplication. Do not be content to say, "I would pray if I could." No, if you cannot pray, pray till you can.'[9]

From what I have just said, you might conclude that I am advocating an austere life of bondage to habit. No! To get back to prayer is to get back to joy. Listen to how David describes his times of prayer: 'You have made known to me the path of life; you will fill me with joy in your presence, with eternal pleasures at your right hand' (Ps 16:11).

Now listen to what the blind hymnwriter Fanny Crosby (1820–1915) wrote:

> O the pure delight of a single hour
> That before thy throne I spend,
> When I kneel in prayer, and with thee, my God,
> I commune as friend with friend.

If you have lost the taste for prayer, begin praying *today*. It is too important an activity and too joyous an activity to postpone any longer.

Praising God in a crisis (6:10)

It may come as a surprise to find the words 'giving thanks' in verse 10. Daniel is walking into a trap that he knows has been set for him and that is intended to result in his gruesome death. And he thanks God!

There is some uncertainty as to whether the word used here should be translated as 'thanks' or as 'praise'. Two of the latest English translations use 'praise' (REB, NRSV). A key Old Testament wordbook explains that this uncertainty could be because general thanks can also be called praise.[10] I do not think it is necessary to make a sharp distinction between thanksgiving and praise.

In the Bible we often see people praising or thanking God in the midst of a crisis. Our passage says that it was Daniel's habit to praise God, and the crisis does not seem to have caused him to alter his usual pattern. Philippians 4:6 states that thanksgiving is an important part of prayers of petition. Paul says, 'Do not be anxious about anything, but in everything, by prayer and petition, *with thanksgiving*, present your requests to God.' The Christians in Jerusalem prayed when they faced their first major crisis — the outlawing of their supreme task, evangelism (Acts 4:24–30). Most of their prayer affirms God's sovereignty in creation and history (vs 24–29). In other words, it was essentially a prayer of praise with something like a postscript (vs 30–31) containing their petition.

Praising God in a crisis helps us realise how God's sovereignty applies to the crisis. Then we will come to accept what Romans 8:28 says, that God will turn the crisis into something good. Praise helps us to trust in him and to maintain our peace and self-control amid the crisis. That is why Romans 8:28 is one of the most important keys to a victorious Christian life. Its truth causes us to face the problems we encounter with hope in God's providence. Such hope challenges the bitterness we might have over the wounds that have been inflicted on us. Daniel's hope enabled him to praise God at a time when we would have expected him to be angry and bitter.

The realisation of God's sovereignty may not come to us at once. I often spend my praise time singing hymns at the piano. I try to separate time for this when I am under a heavy load because of pressures or problems in our ministry. I often find that for the first few hymns I do not sing out the words, even though I read them. My mood is too bad for singing! But as I go on, gradually rays of hope — founded on who God is — break through the dark clouds of gloom in my spirit, and give me a reason to sing.

Let me urge you to battle with God until you can develop the 'Romans 8:28 perspective'. We see this battle going on in the psalmist's life in Psalms 42 and 43, which are actually one psalm. The psalm was written at a time when the psalmist said, 'My tears have been my food day and night' (Ps 42:3). In verse 5 we find him carrying out the battle for the 'Romans 8:28 perspective'. He asks himself, 'Why are you cast down, O my soul? Why so disturbed within me?' (v 5). Then he preaches to himself: 'Put your hope in God' (v 5).

That's the key! Putting our hope in God, looking beyond the gloom with the eyes of faith and saying, 'God will turn it for good.' Next the psalmist says, 'for I will yet praise him, my Saviour and my God' (v 5). Praise is the result of this battle. So the psalmist says he will praise God in the future; that is, when the battle has been completed. But the battle is not yet complete for the psalmist. So he repeats the same promise of praise two more times, in verse 11 and in Psalm 43:5.

A hymn book, the psalms, and the beauty of nature

have been very helpful in my praise life. The Bible seems to encourage using aids to praise and thanksgiving. The prayer of the Jerusalem church, mentioned above, was saturated with Scripture. So were the words of praise Mary and Zechariah spoke before the births of Jesus and John the Baptist (Lk 1:47–55, 68–79). George S. Gunn, in a helpful book on the Psalms, says that 'the collection of Psalms in the Bible was designed, no doubt, with great care and judgment' for the purpose of helping God's people in private and public worship.[11] Willem A. VanGemeren, a commentator of the Psalms, likewise says, 'God... encourages us to use the language of the Psalms in our individual and communal prayers and praise.'[12] The New Testament records some statements of praise about the person and work of Christ that scholars think may have been songs used in the early church.[13]

Aids to praise, such as the Psalms, the hymn book, and the beauty of nature, allow thoughts to enter our minds that should have been there but that have been ignored because our minds are clouded by the pressures of life on earth. Augustine Aurelius (354–430), Bishop of Hippo in North Africa and one of the most influential theologians of all time, has said, 'How my love for God is kindled by the Psalms.' James Gilmour, a Scottish missionary to Mongolia and one of the Christian heroes of the nineteenth century, wrote, 'When I find I cannot make headway in devotion, I open the Bible at the Psalms and push in my canoe, and let myself be carried along in the stream of devotion which flows through the whole book; the current always sets towards God and in most places is strong and deep.'[14]

Bringing our burdens to the Lord (6:11)

Verse 11 says, 'Then these men went as a group and found Daniel praying and asking God for help.' When we are under pressure, one of the best things we can do is to pray. First Peter 5:7 says, 'Cast all your anxiety on him because he cares about you.' When we invite Almighty God to handle our earthly problems and have confidence that he will see us through, there is tremendous relief.

Often I am unable to sleep because of problems in our ministry. Then I decide it is time to bring my burden to the Lord. I do this as a conscious and definite act of prayer. The relief and the subsequent sleep is amazing. The problem may not be over, but I know the Lord will help me through it. Psalm 55:22 says, 'Cast your cares on the LORD and he will sustain you.' The great American President Abraham Lincoln said, 'I have been driven many times upon my knees by the overwhelming conviction that I had nowhere else to go.'[15]

Some people scoff at this type of praying and say it is unworthy of mature Christians. That is surprising in view of how many times the Bible urges us to go to God with our needs. One of my favourite passages is Isaiah 58:9: 'Then you will call, and the LORD will answer; you will cry for help, and he will say: Here am I.' Can you imagine the Lord of all creation saying, 'Here am I' to you? Jesus said plainly, 'Ask and it will be given to you; seek and you will find; knock and the door will be opened to you' (Mt 7:11). James 4:2 says, 'You do not have, because you do not ask God.' The Bible clearly states that God takes a personal interest in our welfare. If we don't tell him when we have problems, we insult him.

One reason people have difficulty asking things from God is that they ask selfishly. James 4:3 goes on to say, 'When you ask, you do not receive, because you ask with wrong motives, that you may spend what you get on your pleasures.'

Another reason people have difficulties is that they lose the perspective of grace. They claim that prayers for ourselves are not noble prayers. But in Christianity we are what we are only because of God's grace. There is nothing noble in us. We are always asking God's help because that's where our help comes from.

So it is no shame to humble ourselves by going to God and asking his help. When the problem is solved, we will not take any glory but will hand it all to Jesus. In the end God is glorified. And because we are intimately united with God, we share some of the joy of that glory. Like a child who is thrilled when his mother is praised for a beautiful song she sang, we are thrilled that our heavenly Father is praised. That thrill is so much more satisfying and lasting than appearing to be noble in the sight of other people whose opinions change constantly.

The 'grace perspective' of prayer is captured well in two quotes from that great preacher of grace, Charles Spurgeon. He said in a sermon, 'Do not reckon you have prayed unless you have pleaded, for pleading is the very marrow of prayer.' In another sermon he said, 'The best style of prayer is that which cannot be called anything else but a cry.'[16]

Christian dissenters are always polite (6:11–20)

The men who found Daniel praying went immediately to the king and reminded him of the decree and the punishment for disobedience (v 12). The king affirmed it saying, 'The decree stands — in accordance with the laws of the Medes and Persians, which cannot be repealed' (v 12). Then they made a serious allegation about Daniel: 'He still prays three times a day.' But before that they reminded the king that Daniel was 'one of the exiles from Judah'. This was a clear challenge to the king's wisdom of giving Daniel such a high position. Then they said, 'Daniel... pays no attention to you, O king, or to the decree you put in writing' (v 13).

You would expect Darius to react to the humiliation with great anger. Instead, verse 14 says, 'When the king heard this, he was greatly distressed; he was determined to rescue Daniel and made every effort until sundown to save him.' The officials, however, drove home the reality of the situation: 'Remember, O king,' they said, 'that according to the law of the Medes and the Persians no decree or edict that the king issues can be changed' (v 15).

When no way to rescue Daniel was found, 'the king gave the order, and they brought Daniel and threw him into the lions' den.' What he said to Daniel as he was being thrown in shows that he respected Daniel for his commitment to his principles: 'May your God, whom you serve continuously, rescue you!' (v 16).

After making sure the den was properly sealed, 'the king returned to his palace and spent the night without eating and without any entertainment being brought to him. And he could not sleep' (v 18). This behaviour suggests that he truly loved Daniel. This is confirmed as we read on: 'At the first light of dawn, the king got up and hurried to the lions' den. When he came near the den, he called to Daniel in an anguished voice, "Daniel, servant of the living God, has your God, whom you serve continuously, been able to rescue you from the lions?"' (v 20).

Clearly the king respected Daniel and loved him deeply. Even after he was humiliated through Daniel's behaviour, the king's respect and affection for Daniel did not diminish. This fits in with other people's reactions to Daniel in this book, too. Daniel distinguished himself as a highly principled and lovable person.

Have you heard people challenge Christians to 'Dare to be a Daniel?' When that is said, what is usually meant is something like, 'Be committed to your principles whatever the cost.' But Daniel distinguished himself not only by steadfast commitment to principle but also by his polite and lovable nature. That should not surprise us, for love is the most important of Christian virtues. In Christianity, *principled* also means *loving*. Paul's advice in Colossians 4:6 is appropriate for all our dealings with those who don't share our convictions: 'Be wise in your behaviour towards non-Christians.... Speak pleasantly to them, but never sentimentally, and learn how to give the proper answer to every questioner' (Phillips).

We would expect a person of prayer like Daniel to be a loving person. Prayer is the supreme expression of our love-relationship with God. It is like a conduit through which love enters our lives. God's love is greater than all the hatred, jealousy, and injustice in the world. Therefore, however bad people may have been to us, we are able, through being in touch with God, to get enough energy to go on loving. If our enemies wish to take away our joy by hurting us, they will fail, for our joy comes from love — the love of God.

STUDY QUESTIONS

6:10   In what situations have God's promises of restoration helped you endure difficult experiences? How can you apply those promises to a situation you now face?

What problems have you faced in maintaining a consistent prayer life? What should you do to overcome those problems?

In what situation in your life do you need to apply the truth of Romans 8:28 (God is sovereign over the situation and will turn it for good)?

What are some ways you can develop the perspective of praise and thanksgiving when you are going through a crisis?

6:11   Do you tend to neglect taking your personal needs to God in prayer? What are some reasons for that neglect?

6:11–20   'In *Christianity* principled also means *loving*.' What situations can you think of where this combination of commitment to principle and love has helped bring glory to God? In what situations has the lack of love by supposedly 'principled' people brought dishonour to God?

CHAPTER

13

Keys to
Powerful Prayer

Daniel 9—10

Many years ago I was at a YFC staff meeting with two visiting speakers from another land. Those present were sharing about the burdens they face in their ministries. I said that, as leader of YFC, I struggle when something goes wrong in the movement or when a staff worker acts in an unchristian way. I often ask whether there has been something wrong with me and with my leadership.

Much to my surprise, the visiting preachers were horrified. They said I should not live under such bondage and that God desires to free us from such attitudes. They prayed for my deliverance from these burdens. That affected me strongly because those preachers are godly and wise people who had a very effective ministry among us.

I have often thought about their response during the years since the incident. Is it wrong for me to get upset and to suffer mental agony when there are problems in our work? I have come to the conclusion that it is not wrong. There were many biblical leaders who went through such agony. Daniel was one such leader. In Daniel 9 and 10, in the middle of a description of visions he received, we have a remarkable glimpse of his inner life. We see Daniel struggling with many issues, but we also see him struggling in prayer. So before discussing Daniel's prophecies, we will look at several keys to powerful praying from Daniel 9 and 10.

Earnest prayer and fasting (9:1-3)

Daniel 9:2 says, 'In the first year of... [King Darius's] reign, I, Daniel, understood from the Scriptures, according to the word of the LORD given to Jeremiah the prophet, that the desolation of Jerusalem would last seventy years' (v 2).

The seventy years had almost ended. In response to this discovery, Daniel prayed for the anticipated restoration. His prayer was one of repentance and pleading. He did not take the promise of restoration for granted. He knew that God's promises were for a righteous nation, and he did not want the promise to be forfeited by the sins of the people.

There is a strong sense of urgency and penitence in his prayer. Verse 3 says, 'So I turned to the Lord God and pleaded with him in prayer and petition, in fasting, and in sackcloth and ashes.' Often when people are in desperate need of God's help they give time for fasting.[1] Often, as here, fasting is associated with penitence and the attempt to turn away God's wrath.[2]

There are many reasons for fasting and many benefits we receive from it in our spiritual lives.[3] In a crisis fasting helps us to focus our attention on the problem and to prepare ourselves spiritually for God's answer. Wesley Duewel says, 'Fasting strengthens your prayer priorities, focuses your prevailing, and enables you to give more uninterrupted concentration to prevailing intercession.'[4] There is so much in this world to distract us from the great priorities of life. Fasting helps us to focus on those priorities.

As we focus on particular needs through prayer and fasting, 'it fires us with increasing earnestness and zeal.'[5] Daniel's earnestness is made clear in verse 3, 'So I turned to the Lord God and pleaded with him in prayer and petition.' The word that is translated as 'pleaded' has the idea of earnestness in it.[6] God usually mediates his blessings through a human agency. Earnest prayer and fasting can be a medium for God's power to break through to this world.

So when we are faced with a big challenge, it is wise to stop our busy activity and give time to fasting and prayer. When the evangelist D. L. Moody felt there was a special need in his evangelistic campaigns, 'he would send word to Moody Bible Institute to call faculty and students to a day of fasting and prayer. Often they would pray until two, three, four, or even five o'clock in the morning.'[7]

There is so much playing with religion today, even in evangelical circles. Entertainment seems to have replaced earnestness in the programme of the church. Getting serious with God through fasting and prayer could be one way to ensure that we don't fall into that trap.

Sharing responsibility for the sin of a people
(9:4–20)

Daniel's prayer is primarily one of confession, as he himself says in verse 4: 'I prayed to the LORD my God and confessed.' But what is surprising is that the confession is in the first person. Verse 5 is representative of the whole prayer: 'We have sinned and done wrong. We have been wicked and have rebelled; we have turned away from your commands and laws.' The words 'we', 'us', 'our', and 'ourselves' appear 43 times in verses 5–19 in the NIV.

Some may think Daniel was using this first person for effect and not really taking responsibility for the sin upon himself. Verse 20 eliminates that idea. It says, 'While I was speaking and praying, confessing *my sin* and the sin of my people Israel... ' He must have been one of the most righteous Jews alive at that time. But when his people failed, he prayed as one who also had failed. In verse 7 he said, 'Lord, you are righteous, but this day we are covered with shame,' showing that he took upon himself the shame of his people.

I think of the times when people talk to me about a problem in our ministry. My first impulse is to try to get off the hook by fixing the blame on someone else. We have become so individualistic in our approach to life that we find it difficult to feel any responsibility for the problems of others in our group. Perhaps this is why the visiting speakers I mentioned in the start of this chapter were so upset by what I had said. In the Bible, however, great prayer warriors, like Moses, took upon themselves the responsibility for the sin of their people. They let themselves be hurt by it as they agonised in prayer.

Zeal for God's name (9:17–19)

Verses 17–19 show that a key reason for Daniel's distress was his commitment to God's name. This commitment emerges as the basis for the pleas he makes. He says, *'For your sake*, O Lord, look with favour into your desolate sanctuary.... Open your eyes and see the desolation of the city *that bears your Name.... For your sake*, O my God, do not delay, *because your city and your people bear your Name.'* Daniel was upset when God's name was dishonoured.

Jesus expressed such an attitude when he cleansed the temple in Jerusalem. After recording that incident, John stated, 'His disciples remembered that it is written: "Zeal for your house will consume me"' (Jn 2:17). The verb 'consume' is in the future tense. But in Psalm 69:9, the source of the quote, it is in the past tense. Some scholars believe that the change to the future tense was because the disciples felt that 'zeal for the temple will destroy Jesus and bring his death.'[8] Jesus was willing to sacrifice his life to take away dishonour that came to the name of the Lord.

Henry Martyn (1781–1812) is one of the most heroic figures in missionary history. After graduating in mathematics from Cambridge University at the top of his class, he shunned the prospect of prosperity in Britain to be a missionary to the Muslims. Once, when he was in Iran, a Muslim told him, 'Prince Abbas Mirza killed so many Christians that Christ from the fourth heaven took hold of Mahomet's skirt to entreat him to desist.'

Martyn says, 'I was cut to the soul at this blasphemy.' The Muslim, observing his distress, asked him what was so offensive about what he had said. Martyn replied, 'I could not endure existence if Jesus were not glorified; it would be hell to me if he were thus to be always dishonoured.' The astonished visitor again asked, 'Why?' and Martyn said, 'If anyone pluck out your eyes, there is no telling *why* you feel pain — it is feeling. It is because I am one with Christ that I am thus dreadfully wounded.'[9]

Like Daniel, Henry Martyn was filled with pain when God was dishonoured. Such passion for God's honour drives us into action. In Daniel's case the action was earnest prayer.

In the early 1990s, the news that prominent Christian leaders had fallen into sin was widely publicised in the media. Often Christians enjoy gossiping about these events. Is that because we have lost our zeal for God's name? Does it not hurt us deeply to know that God has been dishonoured by these actions of his representatives on earth? Because we assume that we are not affected by the events, we separate ourselves from them. If that is the attitude of the Christian population today, we cannot hope for revival. When God's name is dishonoured *we are affected*, because our greatest commitment in life is to God's honour.

If we are aware that God's name has been dishonoured by a leader's actions, we must do all we can to restore God's honour. We must pray earnestly about it. We may need to confront the leader.

Today, we often ignore sin in the lives of leaders because we don't want 'to cause trouble'. But by allowing dishonour to God's name to go unchecked, we may be stifling revival. Few things stifle revival as much as sin in the lives of leaders. It gives other Christians an excuse to live defeated lives. Revival often begins when leaders confess their sins. So when we observe sin in the lives of leaders, let us go to God in earnest prayer and in readiness to act, whatever the cost. Of course, with all people — especially leaders — we act in deep humility.

God can speak to us when we pray (9:20–24)

In verses 20 and 21 Daniel says that, while he was praying, the angel Gabriel came to him. Then he says, 'He instructed me and said to me, "Daniel, I have now come to

give you insight and understanding"' (v 22). Gabriel connects the revelation Daniel is to receive with his prayer: 'As
soon as you began to pray, an answer was given, which I
have come to tell you, for you are highly esteemed' (v 23).
The prophecy of the seventy 'sevens' follows (vs 24–27).
James Montgomery Boice has described this passage as the
'key' to prophetic interpretation and the 'backbone' of
prophecy.[10]

The Bible often says that God speaks to us. Fasting and
prayer could make us receptive to a message from God. In
the Bible God often broke through with an important message or revelation when people gave themselves to fasting
and prayer[11] or just prayer.[12] The Bible says God speaks to us
through visions, dreams, voices, angels, nature, tongues,
prophecy, words of wisdom and words of knowledge.[13]
Perhaps sometimes he speaks through clear impressions in
the mind or through our sanctified imagination.

Because we have the Scriptures, all other means God
uses to speak to us take a subordinate place. But I do not
think there is a scriptural basis for ruling out that God can
speak to us in other ways. We can never be one hundred
per cent sure that such messages are infallible, as we are
about the words of the Bible. So every word that claims to
be from God must be tested to see whether it accords with
what the Bible teaches.

I am aware of the fact that Christians often make foolish decisions after prayer and fasting, saying God clearly
spoke to them or confirmed a decision they had made.
That reminds us that we should be careful about ideas that
come to us when we are in prayer. They may be simply the
product of our imaginations or wandering thoughts. This
is why it is good to seek the wisdom of other Christians
before acting on these supposed 'messages' or 'confirma-
tions' from the Lord.

Yet I have learned to regard with some seriousness those
ideas that come to me when I am praying or reading the
Bible. They could be God's prompting. There have been
times when I have been praying about a problem and suddenly an idea comes that, when implemented, provides
the answer to the problem. Often when I am in deep dis-

tress my devotional Bible reading for the day gives me just the word I need, and with great joy I acknowledge that God has spoken to me to comfort and guide.

Taking on the pain of the people (10:1–19)

Along with the honour of being a recipient of God's special revelation, Daniel experienced great pain. Actually pain goes hand in hand with taking responsibility for the sins of the people.

Daniel 10:1 mentions a revelation Daniel had about two years after the revelation of chapter 9. This is how he acted when he saw the vision about a great war: 'At that time I, Daniel, mourned for three weeks. I ate no choice food; no meat or wine touched my lips; and I used no lotions until three weeks were over.' In verse 8 he says, 'So I was left alone, gazing at this great vision; I had no strength left, my face turned deathly pale and I was helpless.'

Daniel responded in a similar way after the vision of chapter 8: 'I, Daniel, was exhausted and lay ill for several days. Then I got up and went about the king's business. I was appalled by the vision; it was beyond understanding' (8:27). In 10:16–17 Daniel says, 'I am overcome with anguish because of the vision, my lord, and I am helpless. How can I, your servant, talk with you, my lord? My strength is gone and I can hardly breathe.'

Our age is very committed to the importance of looking good. A key to leadership is appearance. Public relations people spend great energy to make leaders look good in public. Imagine how people would respond today if a top leader spent many days in what looked like deep depression!

Daniel could have avoided all this pain by disregarding the implications of what he saw and not taking it so personally. This is what most people do today. But Daniel opened himself to the pain. He made himself vulnerable so that he would be hurt.

This bad mood of Daniel's is not viewed as a weakness or condemned in the Scriptures. On the contrary, the heavenly being who spoke to Daniel commended him. Look at verses 10 and 11: 'A hand touched me and set me trembling on my hands and knees. He said, "Daniel, you... are highly esteemed... " And when he said this to me, I stood up trembling.' Next follows a word of praise for his attitude of prayer: 'Do not be afraid, Daniel. Since the first day that you set your mind to gain understanding and to humble yourself before your God, your words were heard, and I have come in response to them' (v 12). Later, again, Daniel is told, 'Do not be afraid, O man highly esteemed' (v 19).

Daniel had won the esteem of heaven. What better place is there to be esteemed! And what caused him to win that esteem? Verse 12 says it was because he set his mind to gain understanding and to humble himself before his God. In heaven greatness is not putting on a show of knowledge; it is confessing our lack of knowledge and setting our mind to learning. It is not pretending to be a big shot; it is humbling ourselves before God. As the old Puritan saying puts it: 'God has two thrones, one in the highest heaven and the other in the lowliest heart.' Isaiah 57:15 says, 'For this is what the high and lofty one says... "I live in a high and holy place, but also with him who is contrite and lowly in spirit."'

Should we feel sorry for Daniel as he suffers like this? No! God gives him something which makes the suffering not only bearable but also worthwhile. The heavenly messenger tells Daniel, 'Peace! Be strong now; be strong.' Daniel tells us, 'When he spoke to me, I was strengthened.' There is an inner strength the person of God has that cannot compare with the show of strength the people of the world try to project! With this strength we can face life with all its eventualities. When trouble comes, we know that we have One who is greater than the trouble. And this God speaks to us and makes us strong. No wonder the messenger said 'Peace' to him.

Often in the Bible we find God's chosen leaders expressing both their deep hurt over the people and the strength they have in the Lord. When Nehemiah, a responsible government official in Persia, heard about the state of Jerusalem he 'sat down and wept. For some days, [he] mourned and fasted and prayed before the God of heaven' (Neh 1:4). Yet it is from Nehemiah that we get that wonderful statement, 'The joy of the LORD is your strength' (Neh 8:10).

Paul said, 'I face daily the pressure of my concern for all the churches. Who is weak, and I do not feel weak? Who is led into sin, and I do not inwardly burn?' (2 Cor 11:28–29). But that statement appears in 2 Corinthians, most of which is an ecstatic reflection on the glory of the gospel ministry. In Galatians 4:19–20 Paul says, 'My dear children, for whom I am again in the pains of childbirth until Christ is formed in you, how I wish I could be with you now and change my tone, because I am perplexed about you!' Yet, later on he says, 'The fruit of the Spirit is... joy' (Gal 5:22).

We are told that 'during the days of Jesus' life on earth, he offered up prayers and petitions with loud cries and tears to the one who could save him from death' (Heb 5:7). The only example of this type of struggle recorded in the Gospels is Gethsemane, where 'Horror and anguish over-whelmed him', and he said to the three disciples who were with him, 'My heart is ready to break with grief' (Mk 14:33–34, REB). Isn't it strange that earlier that same night Jesus had said that when his joy is in us, our joy will be complete (Jn 15:11)?

Christian joy, which is our strength, is able to coexist with pain. So as God's servants we are not afraid to take upon ourselves the pain of the people we seek to serve. Our joy is deeper than our pain. The peace we have in Christ is deeper than the restlessness we take on over the sins of others. All this is alien in today's society, which is dedicated to making people feel good. But those good feelings come from very unreliable sources. So those who depend on them would be reluctant to take on the agony of the sin and need of others.

By using their criteria for happiness, many people would feel sorry for us. They would call us 'head cases' and recommend that we go for therapy to a psychologist! I wonder whether the weeping prophet, Jeremiah, would have qualified for leadership in today's church. We seem to have imbibed the world's thinking so much that there is no place for weeping prophets among our leadership.

Perhaps you are burdened about something that causes

you great pain. You have a loved one living out of God's will, or you are concerned about something in your church that is displeasing to God; or it breaks your heart to see your nation leaving its moral foundations and sliding along a path to destruction. Don't be afraid to feel pain about this. But first make sure that you have the joy of the Lord to give you the strength to endure that pain.

Let us show the world that there is joy that comes amid costly loving when we derive our strength from Almighty God. And to those suffering over the sin of others, we say, 'Don't feel bad about feeling bad.'

Battling the forces of darkness in prayer
(10:12–13, 20–21)

The messenger tells Daniel something very strange in 10:12–13. He says, 'Since the first day... your words were heard, and I have come in response to them. But the prince of the Persian kingdom resisted me twenty-one days. Then Michael, one of the chief princes, came to help me, because I was detained there with the king of Persia.' The prince of Persia is 'apparently the satanic agent assigned to the sponsorship and control of the Persian realm.'[14] Verse 20 refers to another prince, the prince of Greece.

This is a fairly explicit reference to what are now known as 'territorial spirits'. The belief that there are spirits controlling regions is widely held by the people of Sri Lanka. When travelling to a new region, they often will make a donation at the shrine of the god of the region for protection and blessing. Missionaries describe huge spiritual battles fought with such demons when they go to preach the gospel in an area controlled by demonic forces.[15]

The heavenly messenger tells Daniel that he came in answer to his prayer, but that he was detained for twenty-one days because the prince of Persia resisted him. But the heavenly prince Michael came and helped him, and they were able to overcome the resistance. We can assume that Daniel was praying while this spiritual battle was going on. Paul says that we, too, 'battle against spiritual forces of evil in the heavenly realms' (Eph 6:12). After describing the armour we need to put on for this battle (6:13–17), Paul says, 'And pray in the Spirit' (6:18). The implication is that when we pray we are battling the forces of Satan.

Daniel 10:12–13 implies that, during the twenty-one days that the heavenly messenger was battling the prince of Persia, Daniel was praying. As Gleason Archer says, this passage gives us an example of 'undiscourageable persistence' in prayer.[16] To us there is an encouragement to keep battling in prayer even though answers may not come at once. Jesus said that we 'should always pray and not give up' (Lk 18:1) and went on to illustrate this principle with a parable about a widow who refused to give up when a judge ignored her plea.

Praying is the most powerful thing we do on earth. Let us be faithful at it. It may be prayer for revival. It may be prayer for the conversion of some unbelievers, whom Paul describes as blinded by Satan 'so that they cannot see the light of the gospel of the glory of Christ' (2 Cor 4:4). It may be prayer for the repentance of a child or of a fellow Christian under the grip of Satan. People may not be open to listen to us when we advise them or witness to them. But we can take the battle to a higher plane. We can fight Satan, who holds them in his grip, so that the grip will be loosened and they will be less resistant to the wooing of God's Spirit.

Prayer is exciting! A person involved in biblical praying will never have a dull moment. There will be pain, but there won't be boredom. And think how many people are struggling with boredom today.

Prayer is something you can do when you are physically too feeble for other forms of ministry. In fact, prayer warriors never retire from service. When their physical strength is diminished, they simply get a promotion, so that most of their service is done on the higher plane of battling in prayer.

Don't wait till you are at retirement age to become a prayer warrior. If you are out of touch with prayer, it is unlikely that you will get back in touch after retirement, unless you seriously repent of your prayerlessness. But if you are a prayer warrior now, retirement will hold no terrors for you. You will be delighted at the prospect of giving more time than before to the most powerful thing you can do. Isn't that beautiful? When you are too weak to do physically exerting service, you are freed to be a powerful warrior!

STUDY QUESTIONS

9:1–3   Why is fasting no longer popular among Christians? What can be done to restore it to its place of importance in your life and that of the community to which you belong?

9:4–20   Daniel's taking on responsibility for the sins of his people points to the strong ties of community solidarity advocated in the Scriptures. This is an area where biblical thinking clashes strongly with the individualism of our culture. What blessings of solidarity is the church missing because of its individualism? What can we do to bring back the biblical practice of community solidarity into our church life?

9:17–19   What are some of the things you should be doing, out of zeal for God's name, which some will regard as unnecessary interference in other people's affairs?

9:20–24   Can you recall times when you sensed that God spoke to you? How did it happen? How can you ensure that you are not misled into thinking God has guided you when he has not done so? What do you need to do to be more receptive to his voice?

10:1–19   Would a person like Daniel, who took on himself the pain of his people and expressed it in anguish, feel at home in the Christian community to which you belong? Why or why not?

        In what areas does the love for others cause you pain? What should you do to ensure that the joy of the Lord sustains you amid that pain?

10:12–13, 20–21   What specific problems in your life need to be battled in prayer? How will you carry out that battle?

14

The Mysterious Prophecies of Daniel

Daniel 7—12

'Scholars debate, more fanciful minds revel in speculation, and the ordinary reader tends to look quickly the other way.' Those words of Ronald Wallace introduce his treatment of the second half of the book of Daniel (chapters 7—12). This section describes revelations made to Daniel, primarily about the future, and his responses to them.

Does this section have a place in a book on spiritual living in a secular world? In the previous chapter we saw that it does. If this were a book about predictive prophecy, we would devote more space to the very important prophecies found here. But in this chapter we will look only briefly at these prophecies. In the next chapter we will focus on some themes from these prophecies that apply to us today.

Interpreting apocalyptic literature

The visions in Daniel 7—12 are expressed in a form known as apocalyptic. This comes from the Greek word *apokalupsis*, meaning 'revelation' or 'disclosure'. The word appears in the first verse of the book of Revelation. In fact Revelation is sometimes referred to as 'The Apocalypse'. Daniel is the earliest of the surviving Jewish apocalyptic writings. The other surviving documents are dated between the third century BC and the second century AD.

There is no complete agreement on a definition of apocalyptic literature, but there are some features that appear in these writings that help identify them as apocalyptic. The following list is taken from a chapter by C. M. Kempton Hewitt in a very helpful book on predictive prophecy, *Dreams, Visions and Oracles*:

- All apocalyptic literature focuses on conflict, a conflict always set in the framework of eschatology. By *eschatology* is meant that a second, distinct age, a creation by God, is looming over our present age and will break in upon history at some point in time.
- Almost without exception the revelation takes place through visions and dreams.
- These visions are replete with symbolism, often involving animals and numbers. History is often presented in symbolic images or allegories, so that a master code book may be needed to understand it.
- Angels and demons enter the struggle, often with violent and bloody consequences.
- Usually implicit in the struggle is the portent for the inauguration of a New Age, sometimes associated with a Messiah.
- Apocalyptic writers lived during times of hardship, usually including persecution.
- Overarching the apocalyptic scene is a sense of mystery and urgency.[1]

Because so much of apocalyptic writing is given by means of symbols, the same statement may have a wide variety of interpretations by different Bible students. All too often the explanations of different expositors worthy of respect are mutually exclusive.[2] This is one reason why so many people are afraid to study these sections of Scripture. This, as we shall see in the next chapter, gives reason for humility as we study these passages. Even Daniel once said after a vision that it was 'beyond understanding' to him (8:27).

If Daniel found that the vision he received 'was beyond understanding', do we have any hope of making progress with this material? Is it worth studying the prophecies at all? There are several reasons why all Christians should study these passages and expect to benefit from them.

First, even though we may not be able to interpret the details of all the predictions or accurately identify what particular event is being spoken of in a given text, we *can* understand the trends being predicted, such as the growth and power of evil forces. This point will be discussed in the next chapter.

Second, while we may not be able to identify all the events predicted, we can identify *some* events in many apocalyptic passages. For example, in Daniel 8 the names of some kingdoms are given in the text itself. When working with these prophecies, however, we must keep in mind that different visions can describe the same events. The fact that one vision follows another does not mean that the events in the second vision follow chronologically those predicted in the first.

Third, key themes are repeated in these passages that contain the heart of their message. These can be ascertained without much difficulty by one who reads through the passages carefully. These themes — which are relevant to daily life — are the most important things God wants to communicate to us through the revelations.

When I studied Daniel 7—12 carefully for the first time, I went through the section many times trying to understand what its overall message is. I found five themes that appear often. I coloured the texts, giving each theme a different colour. There were very few sections that were not coloured when I finished this procedure.

The five themes I found in Daniel 7—12 are:

1. How Daniel responds to the situations he faced and the visions he saw. (This discovery gave rise to the previous chapter of this book.)

2. What God's people and institutions will experience in the future.
3. How a powerful kingdom will arise in the future and harm God's people.
4. How that kingdom will be defeated and destroyed.
5. The certainty that God will conquer in the end.

In the remainder of this chapter, as I briefly summarise the contents of the visions, you will see that these themes are the same as the theme of the book of Daniel: *The sovereign Lord rules over history.*

The four beasts, the Ancient of Days, and the Son of Man (7:1–28)

The revelation of Daniel 7 was given during the first year of king Belshazzar's reign, that is about 553 BC. It comes in the form of a vision (vs 2–14) followed by an interpretation of the vision (vs 15–27). It is about four great beasts, which are interpreted as four kingdoms that will rise from the earth. Each kingdom is replaced by the next. The fourth beast is more powerful than the rest and will have many kings, represented by horns. The last of the kings is the most powerful and arrogant, and he will wage war against the saints and defeat them (vs 8, 21). But God, known here as the Ancient of Days, will pronounce judgement in favour of the saints and hand over the kingdom to them (v 22).

This vision mentions 'one like a son of man, coming with the clouds of heaven.' It is said that 'he approached the Ancient of Days and was led into his presence' (v 13). Then follows a description of his authority and power. It is remarkable to see such a description in a Jewish writing about one who is clearly viewed as separate from God. It even says that he is worshipped: 'He was given authority, glory and sovereign power; all peoples, nations and men of every language worshipped him. His dominion is an everlasting dominion that will not pass away, and his kingdom is one that will never be destroyed' (v 14).

By the first century BC 'Son of Man' was being used as a

messianic title.[3] Jesus took the title for himself, and at his trial he directly associated it with the Daniel passage. Responding to the high priest's question of whether he was 'the Christ, the Son of God' he said, 'In the future you will see the Son of Man sitting at the right hand of the Mighty One and coming on the clouds of heaven' (Mt 26:64). He alludes to parts of this Daniel text in several other places, too.[4] As one writer puts it, 'Clearly, Jesus understood this passage as a prophetic portrayal of his own person: his incarnation, ascension, and inheritance of the kingdom of God.'[5]

The ram, the goat, and the horn (8:1–27)

The revelation of Daniel 8 was given during the third year of King Belshazzar's reign, that is, two years after the previous one (v 1). It also comes in the form of a vision (vs 2–14) followed by an interpretation of the vision (vs 15–26).

It starts with a ram with two horns, who was so powerful that he did as he pleased and became great (vs 3–4). Verse 20 says this ram 'represents the kings of Medes and Persia.' He is defeated by a goat with a prominent horn (vs 5–7). The prominent horn is identified as the king of Greece (v 21). At the height of its power this large horn is broken and replaced by four prominent horns (v 8) that, the interpretation says, represent four kingdoms that will emerge from his nation but will not have the same power (v 22).

Out of one of the horns will come another horn that starts small but grows to great power (vs 9–10). This horn is not identified, but the description shows that it is about the Greek (actually Syrian Seleucid) King Antiochus Epiphanes. He took control of Palestine in 168 BC and decided that the Jews were to be assimilated into his Hellenistic (Greek) culture. 'He sent emissaries throughout the land to proclaim that the Jewish religion was proscribed, copies of the Old Testament were to be destroyed, a pig sacrificed on the great altar in the Jerusalem temple, and the temple rededicated to a Greek god.'[6] The first chapter of the apocryphal book 1 Maccabees describes these events vividly.

Daniel 8 predicts these events in verses 11 and 12. The horn 'set itself up to be as great as the Prince of the host [that is, God]; It took away the daily sacrifice from him, and the place of his sanctuary was brought low. Because of rebellion, the host of the saints and the daily sacrifice were given over to it.' Then a holy one is said to ask how long it will take for this vision to be fulfilled (v 13). The answer given is, 'It will take 2,300 evenings and mornings; then the sanctuary will be reconsecrated' (v 14). This is 'the first of Daniel's mysterious numbers, debated for two thousand years.'[7] We will not try to interpret it here. But we know that these events took place and that the sanctuary was restored in 164 BC.

Verse 13 describes the desecration of the temple as 'the rebellion that causes desolation'. In Daniel 9:27, 11:31 and 12:11 we find reference to 'the abomination that causes desolation'. That phrase is used to describe 'a detestable object of pagan idolatry so loathsome to God that his people would feel desolate and devastated in its presence.'[8] In 11:31 it is clearly used to refer to the defiling of the temple by Antiochus. First Maccabees 1:54 also identifies the abomination of desolation with this event. But we will see in the next section that this phrase could be used for other events, too.

The seventy 'sevens' (9:24–27)

The revelation of 9:24–27 is the shortest of the revelations of Daniel 7—12. But it has been described as the 'key' to prophetic interpretation and the 'backbone' of prophecy.[9] The message Daniel received was about seventy 'sevens'. Verse 24 says, 'Seventy "sevens" are decreed for your people and your holy city.' Earlier the sevens were understood as 'weeks', which was the way the King James Version translated it. But many commentators now view that as incorrect. They believe the sevens refer to groups of seven years. Thus seventy sevens would yield 490 years.

Six things are predicted about the people and to their

holy city. The first three deal with taking away sin: (1) 'to finish transgression,' (2) 'to put an end to sin,' and (3) 'to atone for wickedness' (v 24). The next three deal with the establishment of God's kingdom and righteousness: (4) 'to bring in everlasting righteousness,' (5) 'to seal up vision and prophecy,' and (6) 'to anoint the most holy' (v 24).

Verse 25 associates this period with 'the Anointed One': 'Know and understand this: From the issuing of the decree to restore and rebuild Jerusalem until the Anointed One, the ruler, comes, there will be seven "sevens", and sixty-two "sevens".' This adds up to sixty-nine 'sevens' or 483 years.

There is some uncertainty about which decree to rebuild Jerusalem is meant here. But the time approximates to the period between the start of rebuilding and the coming of Christ. The Hebrew word for 'Anointed One', can be translated as 'Messiah' or 'Christ'. Other people were given this title in the Old Testament, but many scholars see this passage as a prophecy about Christ, and I tend to agree.

Some take the seven 'sevens' mentioned first as the period for completing Jerusalem's restoration, and the sixty-two 'sevens' as the period between the restoration and the Messiah's coming to Israel.

Verse 26 says, 'After the sixty-two "sevens", the Anointed One will be cut off and will have nothing.' I take that to refer to the crucifixion. Then 'the people of the ruler who will come will destroy the city and the sanctuary' (v 26). This could be the destruction of Jerusalem in AD 70 by the Roman Emperor Titus.

Verse 27 speaks of 'an abomination that causes desolation' being set up 'on a wing of the temple.' We saw that in 8:13 this phrase referred to the events of 168 BC. But according to the interpretation we are following here, verse 27 should refer to the desecration of the sanctuary in AD 70. Jesus also used this phrase when predicting this desecration of Jerusalem in AD 70 (Mt 24:15). Therefore the acts of Antiochus in 168 BC seem to foreshadow what is to come in the future. In fact its final fulfilment may be the activity of the Antichrist, as we shall see in our discussion of 11:36–37.

The prophecy ends, however, with the hope of triumph.

It says the abomination will be set up 'until the end that is decreed is poured out on him.' Again we see the hope of the book of Daniel: Evil will have its day, and during that time it will be very powerful. But it will finally be decisively defeated.

Antiochus and the Antichrist (11:1–45)

Detailed predictions of history
Daniel 11 and 12 seem to be a continuation of the vision begun in Daniel 10. The revelation of Daniel 11 gives, in some detail, the course of history after the time of Daniel as it affects the Jews. As Joyce Baldwin points out, 'Nowhere else [in the Bible] is prediction as specific and detailed as here.'[10] In fact we have something like a life-history of Antiochus given in advance.

Because this prophecy is so close to history, many scholars say it is actually history written after the events and not what it claims to be — prophecy written before the events. Some take the mediating view that this is a genuine prophecy of Daniel that was worked over and paraphrased in order to make it conform so minutely to the historical events. Yet, given God's ability and foreknowledge, it is not difficult to think that he could have revealed these facts to Daniel before the events in the form given here. Joyce Baldwin says that 'an earthbound rationalistic humanism has so invaded Christian thinking as to tinge with faint ridicule all claims to see in the Bible anything more than the vaguest references to future events.' Her verdict is worth quoting in full:

> Human thought, enthroned, has judged a chapter such as Daniel 11 to be history written after the event, whereas God enthroned, the one who was present at the beginning of time and will be present when time is no more, may surely claim with justification to 'announce from of old the things to come' (Is 44:7).[11]

If you are not familiar with ancient history, you might be baffled by the descriptions in Daniel 11 of various unnamed rulers and their activities. You can, however, see very clearly the theme that rulers come and flourish but soon lose their power. You can also catch the sense of God's sovereignty over history. But if you consult a guide that explains these events, you will be struck by how close the predictions in this chapter are to what really took place. The notes in a study Bible like the *NIV Study Bible* or a one-volume commentary like *The International Bible Commentary* would suffice for this purpose.

From Persian rule to Antiochus

Two hundred years of Persia's rule are passed over in one verse (v 2). This is because 'her rule of the Jews was mainly beneficent' (Millard) and so was not significant for the theme of the vision. Verse 3 introduces the Greek Emperor, Alexander the Great, and verse 4 the breakup of his kingdom after his death. Then the struggles between the north and south in the Greek kingdoms are described (vs 5–20).

Verse 21 introduces Antiochus IV (Epiphanes) who is called 'a contemptible person who has not been given the honour of royalty' (v 21). This is because he was the uncle of the heir to the throne. He was made king because the heir was too young to rule after his father had been assassinated. Verses 22–35 describe Antiochus' career and how he persecuted the Jews. Here we find again that expression 'abomination that causes desolation', as his desecration of the temple is described (v 31).

The Antichrist

At verse 36, without any explicit mention that a new king is being spoken of, we find the vision passing over from Antiochus to a person who does things beyond what Antiochus did. It says, 'The king will do as he pleases. He will exalt and magnify himself above every god and will say unheard-of things against the God of gods.' The next verse says, 'He will show no regard for the gods of his fathers... nor will he regard any god, but will exalt himself above them all.'

Many scholars believe verses 36–45 refer to the Antichrist. In fact, Paul's description of the Antichrist, whom he calls 'the man of lawlessness,' gets its language from Daniel 11:36–37. Paul says, 'He will oppose and will exalt himself over everything that is called God or is worshipped' (2 Thess 2:4). Verses 40–45 describe the last campaign of this king.

His end is described in verse 45: 'He will pitch his royal tents between the seas at the beautiful holy mountain. Yet he will come to his end, and no one will help him.' The holy mountain is probably Jerusalem or Zion. E. J. Young points out that because Antiochus died in Tabae in Persia, this seems to refer to someone else. He says that 'in placing the destruction of the great world power which opposes the people of God near to Jerusalem, Daniel is in harmony with other Old Testament references' (Joel 3:2, 12–16; Zech 14). Young's conclusion is: 'The great final enemy of the people of God, the Antichrist, will make his last stand and will come to his end in territory which is sacred and holy.... His end will be complete, apparently brought about by the glorious return of the Son of God from heaven.'[12] Of course, such a conclusion can be drawn only after reading the New Testament, especially what it says about the Antichrist in 2 Thessalonians and Revelation.

The fact that the king in chapter 11 refers both to Antiochus and to the Antichrist is an example of what is called typology. In typology 'persons, things, or events in the Old Testament [are seen as] foreshadowing or patterns ("types") of persons, things, or events in the New Testament.'[13] The New Testament gives David and Melchizedek as types of Christ. According to this interpretation, Christ would be called the antitype. The antitype always fulfils the characteristics described with greater intensity than the type. So Jesus is greater than David, and the Antichrist is more evil and powerful than Antiochus.

The final triumph of God's people (12:1–13)

Daniel 12 begins with a time of great distress from which the saints — 'everyone whose name is found written in the book' — will be delivered (v 1). Verse 2 gives the first clear reference in the Bible to a resurrection of both the righteous and the wicked: 'Multitudes who sleep in the dust of the earth will awake: some to everlasting life, others to shame and everlasting contempt.'[14] Verse 3 exults in what the saints will finally experience: 'Those who are wise will shine like the brightness of the heavens, and those who lead many to righteousness, like the stars for ever and ever.'

Three times it is said that before the glory there will be times of trial and testing for the saints (vs 1, 7, 10). The question is asked in verse 6: 'How long will it be until these astonishing things will be fulfilled?' The answer given is that 'it will be for a time, times and half a time' (v 7), which probably means a year, two years, and half a year, or three-and-a-half years. This is what 1,290 days in verse 11 roughly adds up to. These days are the period 'from the time that the daily sacrifice is abolished and the abomination that causes desolation is set up.'

But even after that the saints must persevere a few more days. Verse 12 says, 'Blessed is the one who waits for and reaches the end of 1,335 days.' Forty-five days, or a month-and-a-half, is added. These times suggest that the close of the book is intended to help the saints to persevere amid hardship with the hope it will last only for a limited period.

The book ends with a command and a promise to Daniel: 'As for you, go your way till the end. You will rest, and then at the end of the days you will rise to receive your allotted inheritance' (v 13). This is the type of practical advice that is closely connected with the prophecies about the future in the Bible. Our practical response to prophecy is the topic of the next chapter.

This chapter is more difficult than the other chapters of this book. But I trust that as you read it you were struck by the implications of its theme. God knows what is going to happen in history. He is aware of even the most terrible events. And he will not permit anything to happen that he will not use to fulfil his good purposes. He will conquer in the end. And, if this One who holds the future also holds our hand, what a strong reason we have to enjoy peace in our hearts amid all the perplexing things we encounter, and what a strong reason we have to be obedient to God whatever the price.

STUDY QUESTIONS

What thoughts come to your mind as you think about reading the predictive (apocalyptic) passages of Daniel and Revelation? How has the first section of this chapter given you a little more confidence to launch out? Perhaps you should purchase a Bible handbook or one-volume commentary to keep by your side for reference as you read such sections.

7:1–28   What does the description of the Son of Man in this passage (vs 13–14) tell you about the coming Messiah? Why do you think Jesus used this title as one of his favourite ways to refer to himself?

8:1–27;   After reading the summaries of Daniel 8:1–27 and
9:24–27   9:24–27, and after noting that the theme of that book is 'The sovereign Lord rules over history,' how are you able to look at the perplexing events of contemporary history in a new light?

11:1–45   What differences do you see between the normal *predictive prophecy* (which forms most of Daniel 11) and *typology* (which is found in the description of Antiochus and the Antichrist)?

12:1–13   Daniel 12:2 contains the first clear reference to a resurrection of both the righteous and the wicked. This doctrine finds its full expression in the New Testament. This feature of truths being unfolded gradually in the Bible is known as progressive revelation. What other doctrines are revealed progressively in the Bible?

15

Living in the Shadow
of the End Times

Daniel 7—12

We must never forget that the primary rea-
son God gave us prophecies about the future was to help us
live faithfully in the present — not to satisfy our curiosity
about what is going to happen. Jesus' fullest discourse
about the future has been called 'The Little Apocalypse'.
The version in Mark covers 33 verses, and it has nineteen
imperatives (commands or instructions) about how we
should think and act in the light of what is going to happen.[1] The discourse proper starts with the imperative,
'Watch out,' and ends with, 'Watch!' (Mk 13:5, 36).

After discussing the contents of the prophecies of Daniel
7—12 it is appropriate, therefore, to look at how those
prophecies should influence the way we think and act.

Our attitude toward the signs of the times
(8:27; 10:12; 12:9-10)

There is ample evidence that Daniel was not expected to
understand the meaning of all the things he saw and
recorded for posterity. Once after a revelation he said, 'I
was appalled by the vision; it was beyond understanding'

(8:27). Kempton Hewitt points out that 'in both Daniel and Revelation, the writers themselves admit to an overwhelming sense of inadequacy in the face of the awesome visions confronting them.' Therefore, he says, 'Any attempt to understand the apocalypses better must begin with humility and awe.'[2]

In Daniel 10:12 the heavenly messenger tells Daniel why God chose him to receive these messages. He says, 'Since the first day that you set your mind to gain understanding and to humble yourself before your God, your words were heard, and I have come in response to them.' Setting the 'mind to gain understanding' and 'humility' go together here. If all who sought to understand prophecy had such humility, we might have avoided some of the ugly battles over prophetic details that have marred the recent history of the church and brought so much dishonour to Christ.

But aren't we Christians sure about what we believe? Isn't uncertainty about prophecy contrary to the authority of Scripture? Not at all. We can be sure about the things the Bible teaches clearly. In terms of prophecy these would include the following truths:

- Christ will come again in power and glory.
- He will defeat Satan and his forces and gloriously consummate his kingdom.
- Satan and his forces will exert great power before this defeat.
- Christ will judge the world righteously.
- The dead will be raised. The righteous will be raised to everlasting life in heaven and the unrighteous to everlasting damnation in hell.

My point is, that while other items might be included in this list, we can be clear and uncompromising about the fundamentals of the faith given in Scripture. When the Scriptures are silent or only give hints about issues, we must tread cautiously.

A friend of mine said the following about Christians who hold a certain viewpoint about the end times: 'Their ideas may be wrong, but they are sure about what they believe. At a time when there is so much uncertainty about what the Bible teaches, it is refreshing to see a group that is sure about their beliefs.'

Yet our commitment is not to certainty. Our commitment is to truth. Thank God he has given us a book that is true from cover to cover. But there are certain issues that the Bible does not address clearly. It says as much about the end times as we need to know, but it does not answer all our questions. We can be certain about what the Bible clearly teaches, but on other things we should leave room for diversity of opinion and be tentative about our views.

When people preach with complete authority about things the Bible does not clearly state, they are undermining its authority. They proclaim their ideas with the same authority as they proclaim truths clearly taught in the Bible. When their ideas are found to be false, some people might doubt the authority of the Bible, because those ideas were presented as biblical.

For example, we need to be cautious about the time of Christ's return. I have heard and read about people who, based on their study of Scripture or on a revelation God supposedly gave them, affirm that the Lord will return within a given number of years. Some Christians receive their claims with an attitude of awe, partly because those who make these statements are often godly people.

Yet when the disciples asked Jesus, 'Lord, are you at this time going to restore the kingdom to Israel?' he replied, 'It is not for you to know the dates or times the Father has set by his own authority' (Acts 1:7). Earlier he had said, 'No one knows about that day or hour, not even the angels in heaven, nor the Son, but only the Father' (Mt 24:36). We should say, therefore, that on scriptural grounds we refuse to accept as infallible the predictions so confidently made by these godly people.

Then why are so many signs given in the Bible? They are given to help us be watchful, not to get us to speculate about dates. When we see some of the signs being fulfilled, we realise that Christ *could* return today.

That is what we mean by his 'imminent' return. *Imminent*

comes from a Latin word that means 'to overhang'.[3] It can take the idea of an event 'hanging over one's head.'[4] It means that something could happen at any time, and we should be ready for it. A Christian leader was asked what he would do if he found out that Christ was coming the next day. He is reported to have replied that he would live just as he is living today. He was ready for Christ's coming.

We can say with confidence that Christ *could* come in our generation or even today. But we dare not say he *will* come in our generation. When we say that, we are going beyond what the Bible teaches. Revelation 22:18 warns about the dangers of adding to Scripture: 'I warn everyone who hears the words of the prophecy of this book: If anyone adds anything to them, God will add to him the plagues described in this book.'

There are some predictions in the Scriptures, however, that may not have been clear to their writers but that will become clear at the time of their fulfilment. Daniel 12:8–9 implies that: 'I heard, but I did not understand. So I asked, "My Lord, what will the outcome of all this be?" He replied, "Go your way, Daniel, because the words are closed up and sealed until the time of the end."' John Calvin's comment on this is, 'God wished some of his predictions to be partially understood, and the rest to remain concealed until the full period of the complete revelation should arrive.'[5]

Daniel is told, 'Go your way.' That means, 'Inquire no further; leave this matter alone.'[6] If we are uncertain about a future event not clearly revealed in Scripture, we should leave that aside and not go into wild speculation. There is enough work to do in response to those things about which the Scriptures are clear.

If we cannot predict exactly when and how the prophecies will be fulfilled, why did God give us so many signs in the Scriptures? Daniel 12:10 gives us a hint. After describing how evil will increase in the world and the righteous will be purified through trials, the heavenly messenger tells Daniel, 'None of the wicked will understand, but those who are wise will understand.' In the previous verse the messenger had said that 'the words are closed up and sealed until the time of the end.' At the time of the end, when the signs are fulfilled and persecution of the righteous takes place, the wise will read these prophecies and will understand that the terrible things happening were anticipated by God. That will give them confidence as they seek to be faithful to God's ways.

What the signs do, therefore, is to assure us that God is still sovereign. When we see false messiahs performing miracles and leading many astray, we may be baffled at first. But when we remember that this was predicted in the Scriptures, we realise the demonic source of those miracles. When we suffer greatly because we follow God's ways and find that God does not deliver us, we are reminded that the Scriptures speak of the time when 'the power of the holy people has been finally broken' (Dan 12:7). That encourages our obedience, because we know that our defeat is not only temporary but is actually the stepping stone to a great victory.

So we need to read the prophetic passages of the Bible and take note of the signs of the end time. Prophecies about the future can motivate us to live faithfully in the present.

Fear is real, but God's sovereignty is more real

We may be surprised to note Daniel's terrified response to the visions he saw. Different reasons are given for his terror. Once it was the emotional exhaustion caused by seeing a vision and his inability to understand it (8:27). At least twice it was the sight of the glory of heaven and of the awesome nature of the vision (8:17; 10:7–8).

He mentions terror twice in chapter 7. There his fear was clearly in response to what God revealed to him. He says, after the vision, 'I, Daniel, was troubled in spirit, and the visions that passed through my mind disturbed me. I approached one of those standing there and asked him the true meaning of all this' (7:15–16). Then, after he was given the interpretation of the vision, he says, 'I, Daniel, was deeply troubled by my thoughts, and my face turned pale, but I kept the matter to myself' (7:28).

Could it be that Daniel's fear was aggravated by seeing

the suffering the saints will experience? It was in this revelation that he was told that 'the sovereignty, power and greatness of the kingdoms under the whole heaven will be handed over to the saints' (v 27). But before that they will have great trouble. Verse 21 says, 'This horn was waging war against the saints and defeating them.' Verse 25 says, 'He will... oppress the saints... The saints will be handed over to him for a time, times and half a time.' In 12:7, answering the question, 'How long will it be before these astonishing things are fulfilled?' a heavenly messenger describes this same period: 'It will be for a time, times and half a time. When the power of the holy people has been finally broken, all these things will be completed.'

The most vivid description of the trouble the saints go through is in 11:33–35:

> Those who are wise will instruct many, though for a time they will fall by the sword or be burned or captured or plundered. When they fall, they will receive a little help, and many who are not sincere will join them. Some of the wise will stumble, so that they may be refined, purified and made spotless until the time of the end.

These are terrifying passages. The Bible teaches elsewhere also that in the last days, believers are going to have a very difficult time.[7]

Is it wrong for us to be afraid as we think of this tribulation? The Bible often says that we should not be afraid. Jesus, for example, said, 'In this world you will have trouble. But take heart! I have overcome the world' (Jn 16:33). If that is so, why was Daniel commended just when he was in terror? He said on one occasion, 'A hand touched me and set me trembling on my hands and knees.' But the person who touched him told him as he trembled, 'Daniel, you are highly esteemed.' Those words do not seem to have calmed him, for he says, 'And when he said this to me, I stood up trembling' (Dan 10:10–11).

Often the Bible shows God's great servants initially responding to trouble with fear. We see this most in the Psalms. Fear is the natural reaction to danger, and to deny it is unhealthy. When we face fear, however, we should let our belief in God's sovereignty address it. We should remind ourselves of Jesus' words: 'Take heart! I have overcome the world.' We should also remember that the Bible promises that God's sovereignty will be revealed in the midst of our fearful incidents. That can give us the courage to be obedient.

Fear in itself is not a bad thing. In fact, it could be healthy because it alerts us to danger. Jesus said, 'So when you see standing in the holy place the abomination that causes desolation, spoken of through the prophet Daniel — let the reader understand — then let those who are in Judea flee to the mountains' (Mt 24:15–16). Flight is an action associated with fear. But it was the wisest thing to do at the time. It seems that the Christians took Jesus' words to heart, for 'there is reasonably good tradition that Christians abandoned the city [of Jerusalem], perhaps in AD 68, about halfway through the [Roman] siege.'[8] They fled to the transjordan mountains, which Jesus would have meant in this statement, and saved their lives.

Healthy fear drives us to wise and bold action. Hebrews 11:7 says that Noah 'in holy fear, built an ark to save his whole family.' Healthy fear is different from the crippling fear that causes us to recoil from activity. Such fear is *restrictive*. Healthy fear also differs from embittering fear that causes us to be unkind to others. This is the type of fear Nebuchadnezzar had after his dream in Daniel 2. It caused him to order the execution of all his key advisers. Such fear is *destructive*. In contrast, the healthy fear commended in the Bible is *constructive*.

When we confront our fears with our belief in God's sovereignty, we can live in difficult situations. The Bible promises that we will face such situations. Therefore it is wise for us to develop a healthy response to fear.

Our country has gone through many periods of great terror. On a few occasions I have experienced something of this terror. Once was after I wrote a substantial article and sent it to a certain commission. I wrote it during a time when people who held the type of ideas expressed in the article were in danger. Squads of vigilantes were killing people whom they felt were acting against the national interest. After much prayer, our leaders felt that I should write the article. But for a few days after I sent it, I would wake up suddenly at night in a cold sweat, thinking a squad had come to take me. That was the first time I experienced deep terror. But it did not stop me from writing the article.

Another time I experienced fear was after a Youth for Christ staff worker and two volunteers were badly attacked and wounded in a distant town. Someone needed to make a risky trip to bring them home. Considering the tense atmosphere in the land at the time, it was dangerous to bring them through the areas we had to pass. YFC had one vehicle, a van, that was only a few months old. (We usually travel on motorcycles.) We were advised against taking that vehicle, as it could be taken over by terrorists. Some people said that the senior leaders of YFC should not make the trip because, if something happened to us, the movement would really suffer. But would it be fair to send a junior person on such a difficult trip?

As we struggled with the options over a few days, I was extremely tense. My stomach was in knots. Then the decision was made. I would go with my next most senior colleague, and we would use the YFC van. The moment we made the decision, I felt like a big burden had rolled off my back. The tension left me. We had, as a community, come to feel that this was the will of God. We were tense when we did not know God's will. But once we felt we knew it, there was peace, because when we do the will of God we are moving along the stream of his sovereignty. God's will must triumph. It may be through death, for as we saw, Daniel says that many saints will die in the last days. But that death will become a building block in the construction of the eternal kingdom. Eternity will show that it was a triumph.

Those who don't come to grips with fear stand the risk of compromising their commitment in order to avoid fear. That is the great danger of the theologies advocating material and physical prosperity that are becoming increasingly popular in the church today. They tend to ignore the suffering aspect of the Christian life. They leave people unequipped to face the suffering that the Bible says we will surely face. I have seen some people who hold those views leave our land to go to places of relative safety, even though they could have done a great service here. They seem to deduce that because God must 'prosper' them, it could not be God's will for them to stay in these difficult areas. They go to places where it seems certain that 'blessing' will come to them. They have forgotten that, in the Bible, suffering is one of the most honoured blessings conferred on a Christian.

So don't be afraid of fear. Be afraid of disobedience. God is sovereign over history, and those who obey him are moving along the stream that leads to eternal triumph.

Things will get better and worse

The view of history in Daniel 7—12 is both optimistic and pessimistic. Daniel 12:10 says: 'Many will be purified, made spotless and refined, but the wicked will continue to be wicked.' There are instances right through chapters 7—12 of how the power of evil will increase. The full force of evil is going to be unleashed against the saints.[9] But, with that, righteousness is going to be seen in all its glory. The saints 'will be purified, made spotless and refined' through the crisis (see also 11:35).

The Scottish theologian James Denney (1856–1917) says that both the optimist who says the world will get better and the pessimist who says the world will get worse are wrong. Commenting on Paul's teaching on the end times in 2 Thessalonians, he writes, 'It is a progress in which good and evil alike come to maturity, bearing their ripest fruit, showing all they can do, proving their strength to the utmost against each other; the progress is not in good itself or in evil itself but in the antagonism of the one to the other.'[10] In this battle of good and evil the saints will have their commitment tested to the utmost and will display great heroism.

In chapter 6 we said that heroism is a missing feature of contemporary society. Suffering is the matrix out of which heroism is often born. A young Buddhist monk in Sri Lanka, sensing that there was more to life than what he was experiencing, searched after truth until he encountered Christ. His life was transformed, and he committed himself to sharing the gospel with his people. After some years in Bible college, he went with his young wife to an area with very few Christians as an Assemblies of God preacher.

After some years of service, his church had about seventy converts. The people in the area were enraged and sent messages threatening him with death if he did not stop preaching. But he remained faithful to his call. One day, while he was playing with his one-year-old child, a group of men came to see him. He went to the door to meet them, and they first stabbed him and then shot him to death in the sight of his wife, child, and young sister-in-law.

His widow was a Tamil by race, and they had been serving in a Sinhala area. This was a time when Tamil and Sinhala people were in a violent conflict. But she did not leave that area. She stayed on and continued the work begun by her husband. Over the years it has grown, and its congregation has more than doubled. She, too, has received death threats. But she has remained.

Her young sister who viewed the martyrdom is married to a preacher, and they are living in an even more dangerous area, seeking to reach the people there for Christ.

What looked like a great tragedy became a test for that wife and her sister. They came out purified and refined as gold out of the fire. To us they are a great inspiration and example.

We have an incentive to be obedient whatever the cost, for we know that by the testing of our faith, one of life's great ambitions will be fulfilled in us: we will be purified and made like Jesus. The pain will bring us nearer to the Master and make us more like him. If that is the outcome, the price is worth paying.

Awaiting our final reward (12:2–3, 13)

Christlikeness is not the only reward we have for faithfulness. Daniel 12:2–3 describes an eternal reward: 'Multitudes who sleep in the dust of the earth will awake: some to everlasting life, others to shame and everlasting contempt. Those who are wise will shine like the brightness of the heavens, and those who lead many to righteousness, like the stars for ever and ever.' The book of Daniel ends with a word of encouragement to Daniel based on this eternal reward. He is told, 'As for you, go your way till the end. You will rest, and then at the end of the days you will rise to receive your allotted inheritance' (v 13).

Daniel is told, 'Go your way till the end.' He is not to compromise as he sees the costliness of obedience. He is not to be discouraged as he sees the righteous suffer. The prospect of the heavenly reward will be a stimulus to loyalty, a driving force to taking on the cup of suffering. This is a theme repeated often in the Bible. At the end of Paul's great chapter on the Resurrection, 1 Corinthians 15, he says, 'Therefore, my dear brothers, stand firm. Let nothing move you. Always give yourselves fully to the work of the Lord, because you know that your labour in the Lord is not in vain' (v 58).

Some people scoff at this type of motivation to godliness, saying it is unworthy of the gospel. Jesus did not think so. He said, 'Do not store up for yourselves treasures on earth, where moth and rust destroy, and where thieves break in and steal. But store up for yourselves treasures in heaven, where moth and rust do not destroy, and where thieves do not break in and steal.' Jesus immediately explained why this motivation is so important: 'For where your treasure is, there your heart will be also' (Mt 6:19–21). Paul says the same thing in Colossians 3:2, 'Set your minds on things above, not on earthly things.'

If our treasure is down here, we will not want to sacrifice it for the sake of godliness. We will not want to give it away in order to help others. We will always be comparing ourselves with others and trying to get more treasure, even at the cost of eternal treasure. Jesus knows our natural inclinations. He knows that rational beings consider the profitability of an action before doing it. He addresses this legitimate concern by telling us never to forget heaven. This heavenly perspective will make us heroes on earth. It will impel us to give ourselves in costly service to our fellow humans.

I will end this book with a story that has greatly influenced my life. It is about Dr Brackett, a medical practitioner who lived in a small town in the southern part of the United States. He specialised in serving people who had no money. He would get up on the coldest night and go for miles to help a needy person. His office was on the main street over a clothing store, and there was a plate at the doorway announcing the office.

He never married. He fell in love, but on the day of his wedding he was called out to deliver a Mexican baby. I suppose he had to go to save the life of the mother and child, as there were no other doctors nearby. But his bride gave him up. She said that a man who would fail to appear at his wedding for the sake of a poor person's child would not be any good as her husband. A lot of people agreed with her — but not the parents of the little Mexican child.

Dr Brackett was over seventy years old when he died. After a grand funeral the townsfolk began to argue about the best tombstone they should erect to this wonderful man. But, as often happens, it all ended in talk. The only people who seemed to be worried were the parents of the boy he had delivered so many years earlier.

They were too poor to put up a tombstone. So they took the brass plate announcing the office from the door of the building and placed it on the tomb. An undertaker passing through the cemetery first noticed it. Embedded in a mass of flowers, he read the old inscription:

Dr Brackett
Office upstairs.[11]

Most people would have thought the doctor was a fool for sacrificing earthly success for the sake of service to the poor. But he had an office upstairs, and that made the price he paid worth it all.

STUDY QUESTIONS

8:27; 10:12;   How do you respond when a preacher says he does
12:9–10   not know the full meaning of some prophetic
passages? How do you respond to the statement,
'When people preach with complete authority about
things the Bible does not clearly state, they are
undermining its authority'?

A primary purpose of prophetic signs is to help us
remain faithful amid suffering. Is that the way
Christians usually view signs? Explain. How might
Christians have developed an unbiblical understanding
of signs because they have not taken seriously the
call to suffer?

Fear and   Have you included suffering and healthy fear into
Sovereignty   your way of thinking about life? How has the church
been impoverished today by the neglect of the
doctrine of Christian suffering?

Things Will   Give an example of the statement: 'Suffering is the
Get Better   matrix out of which heroism is often born.' Suffering
and Worse   fulfils one of life's great ambitions — becoming like
Jesus. Why might many Christians find it difficult to
endure suffering if becoming like Jesus is not their
great ambition in life?

12:2–3, 13   How important a motivation is the heavenly reward
to you? How often do you think about 'things above'
(Col 3:2)? Has the heavenly perspective helped you to
combat the subtle temptations to materialism which
come your way?

Endnotes

Chapter 1: Getting Involved in a Fallen World
(Daniel 1:1–8, 17)

1 John Pollock, *Wilberforce* (Herts and Belleville, Mich.: Lion Publishing, 1977), pp 37–39.
2 Cited in F. F. Bruce, *The Book of Acts*, Revised Edition, The New International Commentary on the New Testament (Grand Rapids, Mich.: Wm. B. Eerdmans Publishing Co., 1988), p 271.
3 W. M. Ramsay, *The Bearing of Recent Discovery on the Trustworthiness of the New Testament* (London: Hodder & Stoughton, 1915), pp 35–52.
4 A. R. Millard, 'Daniel', *The International Bible Commentary*, Revised Edition, F. F. Bruce and others, editors (Grand Rapids, Mich.: Zondervan Publishing House, 1986), p 853.
5 D. S. Russell, *Daniel*, The Daily Study Bible (Philadelphia: Westminster Press, 1981), p 24.
6 Ronald S. Wallace, *The Message of Daniel* (Leicester, England, and Downers Grove, Ill.: Inter-Varsity Press, 1979), p 42.
7 Mark Hatfield, *Conflict and Conscience* (Waco, Tex.: Word Books, 1971), pp 104–105.
8 David S. Short, *Medicine as a Vocation* (Nilgiris, India: EMFI; London: Christian Medical Fellowship, 1987), p 39.
9 Joyce G. Baldwin, *Daniel*, The Tyndale Old Testament Commentaries (Leicester, England, and Downers Grove, Ill.: Inter-Varsity Press, 1978), p 80.
10 Harry Blamires, *The Christian Mind* (London: SPCK, 1963; Ann Arbor, Mich.: Servant Books, 1978), p 70.

11 John Stott, *Decisive Issues Facing Christians Today* (Old Tappan, New Jersey: Revell, 1990).

12 John R. W. Stott, *Between Two Worlds: The Art of Preaching in the Twentieth Century* (Grand Rapids, Mich.: Wm. B. Eerdmans Publishing Co., 1982).

Chapter 2: Living out Our Commitment in Daily Life *(Daniel 1:8–21)*

1 Quoted in Stephen Neill, *A History of Christian Missions* (Middlesex: Penguin Books, 1964), p 386.

2 John Wesley, *Wesley's Notes on the Bible*, edited by G. Roger Schoenhals (Grand Rapids, Mich.: Zondervan Publishing House, 1987), p 486.

3 Tom Landry with Gregg Lewis, *Tom Landry, An Autobiography* (Grand Rapids, Mich.: Zondervan Publishing House, 1990), p 173.

4 Ruth A. Tucker, *From Jerusalem to Irian Jaya* (Grand Rapids, Mich.: Zondervan Publishing House, 1983), chap. 9, pp 231–254.

5 This is done in John Piper's book, *Desiring God* (Portland, Ore.: Multnomah Press, 1986).

Chapter 3: Peaceful Living in a Stressful World *(Daniel 2:1–16)*

1 Wayne Grudem, *The First Epistle of Peter*, Tyndale New Testament Commentaries (Grand Rapids, Mich.: Wm. B. Eerdmans Publishing Co.; Leicester, England: Inter-Varsity Press, 1988), p 153.

2 Charles H. Spurgeon, *Spurgeon at His Best*, compiled by Tom Carter (Grand Rapids, Mich.: Baker Book House, 1988), pp 323–324.

Chapter 4: It Happens in Small Groups *(Daniel 2:17–23)*

1 C. S. Lewis, *The Letters of C. S. Lewis to Arthur Greeves, 1914–1963*, edited by Walter Hooper (New York: Collier/ Macmillan, 1986), p 477.

2 Lewis himself wrote thirty-four more books. The rest are compilations of his shorter writings, edited by others and published posthumously.

3 Kathryn Ann Lindskoog, *C. S. Lewis: Mere Christian* (Glendale, Calif.: Regal Books, G/L Publications, 1973), p 1.

4 Richard Lovelace, *Dynamics of Spiritual Life* (Downers Grove: InterVarsity Press, 1979), p 370.

5 John Pollock, *Wilberforce*, p 177.

6 Lovelace, *Dynamics*, p 370.

7 Michael Hennell, *William Wilberforce* (London: Church Book Room Press Ltd., n.d.), p 24.

8 I have dealt with the topic of Christian friendship in detail in my book, *Reclaiming Friendship* (Scottdale, Penn.: Herald Press, 1993; Leicester, England: Inter-Varsity Press, 1991).

9 Lovelace, *Dynamics*, p 370.

10 See Psalm 22:25; 34:3; 35:18 and Ronald S. Wallace, 'Praise', *New Bible Dictionary*, Second Edition, edited by J. D. Douglas, et al. (Leicester, England: Inter-Varsity Press; Wheaton, Ill.: Tyndale House Publishers, 1982), p 957.

Chapter 5: **The Call to Personal Witness** *(Daniel 2:24–49)*

1 John Pollock, *Wilberforce*, pp 66–67.

2 Leighton Ford, *Good News Is for Sharing* (Elgin, Ill.: David C. Cook, 1977), p 123.

3 John R. W. Stott, *Our Guilty Silence* (Downers Grove, Ill.: Inter-Varsity Press, 1967), p 59.

4 I have demonstrated this in my book, *The Christian's Attitude Toward World Religions* (Wheaton, Ill.: Tyndale House Publishers, 1987), chap. 12, 'Uniqueness and Arrogance'.

5 Pollock, *Wilberforce*, p 211.

6 Derek Kidner, *Psalms 73—150*, Tyndale Old Testament Commentaries (Leicester, England, and Downers Grove, Ill.: Inter-Varsity Press, 1975), p 404.

7 Pollock, *Wilberforce*, p 212.

8 A. R. Millard, 'Daniel', p 855.

9 E. M. Blaiklock, *The Acts of the Apostles*, Tyndale New Testament Commentaries (Leicester, England: Inter-Varsity Press; Grand Rapids, Mich.: Wm. B. Eerdmans Publishing Co., 1959), p 140.

10 'Book of Daniel', *Baker Encyclopedia of the Bible*, vol. 1., edited by Walter A. Elwell (Grand Rapids, Mich.: Baker Book House, 1988), p 575.

11 Ronald S. Wallace, *The Message of Daniel*, p 60.

12 See Joyce G. Baldwin, *Daniel*, p 94.

Chapter 6: **Commitment: the Key to Heroism**
(Daniel 3:1–18)

1 Stephen Neill, *A History of Christian Missions*, pp 299–300.

2   From a quote by David Augsburger in *Living Quotations for Christians*, edited by Sherwood Eliot Wirt and Kersten Beckstrom (New York: Harper & Row Publishers, 1974), p 34.
3   Robert A. Anderson, *Signs and Wonders: A Commentary on the Book of Daniel*, International Theological Commentary (Grand Rapids, Mich.: Wm. B. Eerdmans Publishing Co., 1984), p 33.
4   *Spiritual Secrets of George Mueller*, selected by Roger Steer (Wheaton, Ill.: Harold Shaw Publishers; Robesonia, Penn.: OMF Books, 1985), p 72.
5   See Jay Kesler, Foreword to *My Times Are in His Hands* (Singapore: Singapore Youth for Christ, 1991), p 1.
6   Carl F. H. Henry, *Christian Countermoves in a Decadent Culture* (Portland, Ore.: Multnomah Press, 1986), p 51.
7   Elmer L. Towns, *The Christian Hall of Fame* (Grand Rapids, Mich.: Baker Book House, 1971), p 112.

Chapter 7: God is with Us *(Daniel 3:19–30)*

1   John Goldingay makes this point, following a commentator of an earlier generation, J. Kennedy (*Daniel*, Word Biblical Commentary [Dallas, Tex.: Word Books, 1989], p 75).
2   Copyright C. Austin Miles, The Rodeheaver Co.
3   Carl F. H. Henry, *Confessions of a Theologian* (Waco, Tex.: Word Books, 1986), p 113.
4   Sherwood Eliot Wirt, *The Social Conscience of the Evangelical* (New York: Harper & Row Publishers, 1968), p 47.
5   Carl F. H. Henry, *The Uneasy Conscience of Modern Fundamentalism* (Grand Rapids, Mich.: Wm. B. Eerdmans Publishing Co., 1947), p 60.
6   F. W. Boreham, *Mushrooms in the Moor*, cited in *Daily Readings from F. W. Boreham*, selected and arranged by Frank Cumbers (London: Hodder & Stoughton, 1976), p 297.

Chapter 8: Confronting the Powerful with God's Power *(Daniel 4:1–18)*

1   Joyce G. Baldwin, Daniel, p 110.
2   Edward J. Young, *The Prophecy of Daniel* (Grand Rapids, Mich.: Wm. B. Eerdmans Publishing Co., 1949), p 100.
3   Edward J. Young, *Daniel*, p 100.
4   Matthew Henry, *Commentary on the Whole Bible in One Volume*, edited by Leslie F. Church (Basingstoke: Marshall Pickering, reprint of 1960 edition), p 1089.

5   R. A. Torrey, *Personal Work*, Part I of *How to Work for Christ* (Old Tappan, N.J.: Fleming H. Revell Company, n.d.), p 52.

6   Sherwood Eliot Wirt and Kersten Beckstrom, *Living Quotations for Christians*, p 188.

Chapter 9: Witnessing to the Powerful *(Daniel 4:19–37)*

1   J. C. Pollock, *Shaftesbury — The Poor Man's Earl* (London: Falcon Books, 1961), p 3.

2   J. C. Pollock, *Shaftesbury*, p 5.

3   Ingvar Haddal, *John Wesley* (Nashville: Abingdon Press, originally published in 1961 by Epworth Press), p 28.

4   A. R. Millard, 'Daniel', p 858.

5   I have dealt with this in some detail in my book, *The Christian's Attitude Toward World Religions* (Wheaton, Ill.: Tyndale House Publishers, 1987), chap. 11, 'Persuasion and Intolerance'.

6   R. A. Torrey, *Personal Work*, from the cover.

7   The most comprehensive listing of Scripture texts on poverty that I hae seen is in Ron Sider's book, *Cry Justice! The Bible on Hunger and Poverty* (New York: Paulist Press; Downers Grove, Ill.: InterVarsity Press, 1980).

8   See Donald W. Dayton's book, *Discovering an Evangelical Heritage* (New York: Harper & Row Publishers, 1976).

9   Richard F. Lovelace, *Dynamics of Spiritual Life* (Downers Grove, Ill.: InterVarsity Press, 1979), pp 370–371.

10 *Pornography: A Human Tragedy* (Wheaton, Ill.: Christianity Today, Inc., and Tyndale House Publishers, 1986), pp 24, 25.

11 Leighton Ford, *Good News Is for Sharing* (Elgin, Ill.: David C. Cook Publishing Co., 1977), p 49.

12 This story is recorded in Ron Lee Davis, *Gold in the Making* (Nashville, Tenn.: Thomas Nelson Publishers, 1983), pp 101–102.

Chapter 10: People Who Don't Care about God *(Daniel 5:1–31)*

1   Cuneiform is the name given to 'wedge-shaped script written with a sharp instrument on tablets of soft clay, which were then baked, or carved on stone. This method of writing was used by the Sumerians, Akkadians, Babylonians, Assyrians, and other ancient Near Eastern peoples' (F. B. Huey, Jr. and Bruce Corley, *A Student's Dictionary of Biblical and Theological Studies* [Grand Rapids, Mich.: Zondervan Publishing House, 1984], p 482).

2 A. R. Millard, 'Daniel', p 848.
3 Gleason L. Archer, Jr., *Daniel*, The Expositor's Bible Commentary, vol. 7, ed. Frank E. Gaebelein (Grand Rapids, Mich.: Zondervan Publishing House, 1985), pp 69–70.
4 Archer, *Daniel*, pp 69–70.
5 Joyce G. Baldwin, *Daniel*, p 120.
6 Ronald S. Wallace, *The Message of Daniel*, p 95.
7 P. E. Hughes, 'Means of Grace', *Evangelical Dictionary of Theology*, edited by Walter A. Elwell (Grand Rapids, Mich.: Baker Book House, 1984), p 482.
8 I am following the concise comments given by A. R. Millard in this explanation.
9 I have dealt with many issues relating to proclaiming the message of judgement in my book, *Crucial Questions About Hell* (Eastbourne: Kingsway Publications, 1991).

Chapter 11: When Good People Come under Fire
(Daniel 6:1–10)

1 Cited in Warren Wiersbe and Lloyd M. Perry, *Wycliffe Handbook of Preaching and Preachers* (Chicago: Moody Press, 1984), p 185; from Bramwell Booth, *Echoes and Memories*, p 27.
2 J. C. Whitcomb, *Darius the Mede* (Grand Rapids: William B. Eerdmans Publishing Co., 1959), p 8. Cited by Joyce G. Baldwin.
3 D. J. Wiseman and others, *Notes on Some Problems in the Book of Daniel* (London: Tyndale Press, 1965).
4 In *Darius the Mede*.
5 The reader is directed to pages 23–28 of Joyce G. Baldwin's commentary on Daniel for a concise statement on the identity of Darius the Mede.
6 Cited in *Wycliffe Handbook of Preaching and Preachers* (Chicago: Moody Press, 1984), p 185; from *Echoes and Memories*, p 8.
7 From Daniel 1:21 we can infer that the events of Daniel 6 took place in the first year of King Cyrus which is dated at 539 BC. This is about 66 years after his recruitment as a youth by Nebuchadnezzar around 605 BC (see Joyce G. Baldwin, *Daniel*, p 85). If he was 16 years at that time, then he would be 82 years old in Cyrus' first year.
8 Luke 1:6; Acts 24:16; 1 Corinthians 10:32; 2 Corinthians 6:3; 8:20; Philippians 2:15; 1 Thessalonians 2:10; 1 Timothy 3:2, 10; 5:7; Titus 1:6–7; James 1:27.
9 A second reason was the love he felt for the Scriptures and the constant recuperative power they exercised on his whole

being. The third reason was the happiness he felt in God and his work. Taken from Arthur Pierson, *George Mueller of Bristol* (Loiseaux Brothers, Inc.).

10 Colson's story is told in his book, *Born Again* (Old Tappan: Fleming H. Revell Co., 1976).

11 John Calvin, *A Commentary on Daniel*, vol. 1, translated and edited by Thomas Myers (London: The Banner of Truth Trust, 1966 reprint of 1852 edition), p 353.

12 In the NRSV and some other translations the order is reversed, and negligence is mentioned before corruption.

13 Francis Brown, S. R. Driver and Charles A. Briggs, *A Hebrew and English Lexicon of the Old Testament*, based on the Lexicon of William Gesenius (London: Oxford University Press, 1953), p 1115.

14 Joyce G. Baldwin, *Daniel*, p 128.

Chapter 12: Facing Trouble through Prayer
(Daniel 6:10–28)

1 Hatfield, *Conflict and Conscience*, p 163.

2 Charles H. Spurgeon, *Spurgeon at His Best*, compiled by Tom Carter (Grand Rapids, Mich.: Baker Book House, 1988), p 143.

3 1 Kings 8:54; Ezra 9:5; Psalm 95:6; Luke 22:41.

4 Luke 18:11, 13; John 11:41.

5 Matthew 26:39.

6 Matthew 11:25–26; John 12:27–28.

7 Vance Hanver, *The Vance Hanver Quote Book*, compiled by Dennis J. Hester (Grand Rapids, Mich.: Baker Book House, 1986), p 166.

8 From E. Stanley Jones, *How to Pray* (1943), cited in *Selections from E. Stanley Jones*, compiled by James K. Matthews and Eunice Jones Matthews (Nashville, Tenn.: Abingdon Press, 1972), p 132.

9 Spurgeon, *Spurgeon at His Best*, p 143.

10 *Theological Wordbook of the Old Testament*, volume two, edited by R. Laird Harris and others (Chicago: Moody Press, 1980), p 1029.

11 George S. Gunn, *Singers of Israel* (London: Lutterworth Press; Nashville, Tenn.: Abingdon Press, 1963), pp 13–14.

12 Willem A. VanGemeren, *Psalms*, The Expositor's Bible Commentary, vol. 5, ed. Frank E. Gaebelein (Grand Rapids, Mich.: Zondervan Publishing House, 1991), p 5.

13 Colossians 1:15–20; Philippians 2:6–11; 1 Timothy 3:16. See Ralph P. Martin, *Worship in the Early Church* (Grand Rapids,

Mich.: Wm. B. Eerdmans Publishing Co., 1975; London: Marshall, Morgan and Scott, 1964), pp 39–52.

14 The quotes from Augustine and Gilmour are from Gunn, *Singers of Israel*, p 15.

15 Quoted in Hatfield, *Conflict and Conscience*, pp 162–163.

16 Spurgeon, *Spurgeon at His Best*, pp 143–145.

Chapter 13: Keys to Powerful Prayer *(Daniel 9—10)*

1 Judges 20:26; 1 Samuel 7:6; 2 Samuel 12:16–20; Ezra 8:21–23; Nehemiah 1:4, etc.

2 Nehemiah 9:1; Ezra 10:1–6.

3 For a listing of reasons for fasting and the blessings that accrue from it, see David Tripp, 'Fasting', *The Westminster Dictionary of Christian Spirituality*, edited by Gordon S. Wakefield (Philadelphia: The Westminster Press, 1983), p 148, and Wesley L. Duewel, *Mighty Prevailing Prayer* (Grand Rapids, Mich.: Zondervan Publishing House, 1990), pp 187–190.

4 Duewel, *Mighty Prevailing Prayer*, p 188.

5 Duewel, *Mighty Prevailing Prayer*, p 190.

6 Leonard J. Coppes in *Theological Wordbook of the Old Testament*, edited by R. Laird Harris and others (Chicago: Moody Press, 1980), p 126.

7 Wesley L. Duewel, *Touch the World Through Prayer* (Grand Rapids, Mich.: Zondervan Publishing House, 1986), p 96.

8 Raymond E. Brown, *The Gospel According to John I–XII*. The Anchor Bible (New York: Doubleday & Company, 1966), p 124. F. F. Bruce also makes this suggestion in his commentary on John.

9 Constance E. Padwick, *Henry Martyn, Confessor of the Faith* (New York: George H. Doran Company, 1922), p 264.

10 James Montgomery Boice, *Daniel: An Expositional Commentary* (Grand Rapids, Mich.: Zondervan Publishing House, 1989), pp 103–104.

11 Exodus 34:28; Deuteronomy 9:9, 18; Acts 13:2.

12 Acts 10:9–10.

13 See Joyce Huggett, *Listening to God* (London: Hodder & Stoughton, 1986).

14 Gleason L. Archer, Jr., *Daniel*, p 125.

15 See Timothy Warner, 'Power Encounter with the Demonic' in *Evangelism on the Cutting Edge*, ed. Robert E. Coleman (Old Tappan, N.J.: Fleming H. Revell Co., 1986), pp 89–101, and Timothy M. Warner, *Spiritual Warfare* (Wheaton: Crossway Books, 1991).

16 Gleason L. Archer, Jr., *Daniel*, p 125.

Chapter 14: The Mysterious Prophecies of Daniel
(Daniel 7—12)

1 C. M. Kempton Hewitt, 'Guidelines to the Interpretation of Daniel and Revelation', *Dreams, Visions and Oracles*, eds. Carl Edwin Armerding and W. Ward Gasque (Grand Rapids, Mich.: Baker Book House, 1977), pp 103–104.

2 H. L. Ellison makes this point in *Men Spake from God* (Exeter: The Paternoster Press, 1966), p 144.

3 E. J. Young says it occurs 14 times in Enoch 37–71. Enoch is the leading Jewish apocalyptic book, and is a collection of writings dated in the last two centuries BC. See Edward J. Young, *The Prophecy of Daniel*, p 155.

4 Matthew 16:27; 19:28; 24:30; 25:31.

5 'Son of Man', *Baker Encyclopedia of the Bible*, vol. 2, p 1983.

6 G. E. Ladd, *The Last Things* (Grand Rapids, Mich.: William B. Eerdmans Publishing Co., 1978), pp 58–59.

7 A. R. Millard, 'Daniel', pp 862.

8 Morris A. Wiegelt, 'Abomination of Desolation', *Baker Encyclopedia of the Bible*, vol. 1, p 10.

9 James Montgomery Boice, *Daniel: An Expositional Commentary* (Grand Rapids, Mich.: Zondervan Publishing House, 1989), pp 103–104.

10 Joyce G. Baldwin, *Daniel*, p 184.

11 Joyce G. Baldwin, *Daniel*, p 185.

12 Edward J. Young, *The Prophecy of Daniel*, p 253.

13 F. B. Huey, Jr., and Bruce Corley, *A Student's Dictionary for Biblical and Theological Studies* (Grand Rapids, Mich.: Zondervan Publishing House, 1983), p 193.

14 *NIV Study Bible* (Grand Rapids, Mich.: Zondervan Publishing House, 1985), p 1318.

Chapter 15: Living in the Shadow of the End Times
(Daniel 7—12)

1 'The discourse is actually structured and sustained by the nineteen imperatives found in verses 5–37.' William L. Lane, *Commentary on the Gospel of Mark*, The New International Commentary on the New Testament (Grand Rapids, Mich.: William B. Eerdmans Publishing Co., 1974), p 446.

2 C. M. Kempton Hewitt, 'Guidelines to the Interpretation of Daniel and Revelation', p 102.

3   Ernest Weekley, *An Etymological Dictionary of Modern English*, vol. 1 (New York: Dover Publications, Inc., 1967), p 747.
4   *The Shorter Oxford English Dictionary*, vol. 1 (Oxford: Clarendon Press, 1973), p 1026.
5   John Calvin, *A Commentary on Daniel*, Vol. 2, translated and edited by Thomas Myers (London: The Banner of Truth Trust, 1966 reprint of 1853 edition), p 386.
6   Edward J. Young, *The Prophecy of Daniel*, p 260.
7   Matthew 24:9–25; Revelation 13:7–10, 15–17.
8   D. A. Carson, *Matthew*, The Expositor's Bible Commentary, vol. 8, ed. Frank E. Gaebelein (Grand Rapids, Mich.: Zondervan Publishing House, 1984), p 501.
9   Daniel 7:21, 25; 8:12; 11:30–35; 12:7, 10.
10 James Denney, *1 and 2 Thessalonians*, Expositors Bible Commentary (London: Hodder & Stoughton, 1892), pp 313–314. Cited by Ronald S. Wallace.
11 Taken almost verbatim from *Daily Readings from W. E. Sangster*, edited by Frank Cumbers (London: Epworth Press, 1966), p 163.